Collins

Mission: français

Workbook 3

Oliver Gray

Series Editor: Linzy Dickinson

William Collins's dream of knowledge for all began with the publication of his first book in 1819. A self-educated mill worker, he not only enriched millions of lives, but also founded a flourishing publishing house. Today, staying true to this spirit, Collins books are packed with inspiration, innovation and practical expertise. They place you at the centre of a world of possibility and give you exactly what you need to explore it.

Collins. Freedom to teach.

Published by Collins
An imprint of HarperCollins*Publishers*
The News Building
1 London Bridge Street
London
SE1 9GF

Browse the complete Collins catalogue at
www.collins.co.uk

10 9 8 7 6 5 4 3 2

ISBN-13 978-0-00-751346-8

British Library Cataloguing in Publication Data
A Catalogue record for this publication is available from the British Library.

Commissioned by Katie Sergeant
Series concept by Linzy Dickinson
Project managed by Elektra Media Ltd
Development edited by Naomi Laredo
Copy-edited by Claire Trocmé
Concept design by Elektra Media Ltd
Illustrations by Elektra Media Ltd
Typeset by Jouve India Private Limited
Cover design by Angela English

Printed and bound by CPI Group (UK) Ltd,
Croydon, CR0 4YY

Acknowledgements
The publishers wish to thank the following for permission to reproduce photographs. Every effort has been made to trace copyright holders and to obtain their permission for the use of copyright materials. The publishers will gladly receive any information enabling them to rectify any error or omission at the first opportunity.

(t = top, c = centre, b = bottom, r = right, l = left)

Cover tl Dudarev Mikhail/Shutterstock, cover tr Ivonne Wierink/Shutterstock, cover ct ilolab/Shutterstock, cover cb Pack-Shot/Shutterstock, cover b Samo Trebizan/Shutterstock, p 7 tl Digital Media Pro/Shutterstock, p 7 bl Halfpoint/Shutterstock, p 7 tr Jorg Hackemann/ Shutterstock, p 7 br Faraways/Shutterstock, p 8 CandyBox Images/Shutterstock, p 12 Brent Hofacker/Shutterstock, p 18 tl constucter/Shutterstock, p 18 tc Tracy Whiteside/ Shutterstock, p 18 tr Simone van den Berg/Shutterstock, p 18 bl littlewormy/Shutterstock, p 18 bc Antonio Guillem/Shutterstock, p 18 br sebra/Shutterstock, p 21 tl Andrey Popov/Shutterstock, p 21 tc Suzanne Tucker/Shutterstock, p 21 bl John Leung/Shutterstock, p 21 bc Sergey Furtaev/Shutterstock, p 21 br abd/Shutterstock, p 21 tr Maridav/Shutterstock, p 25 tt pictore/iStock, p 25 t duncan1890/iStock, p 25 tc wynnter/iStock, p 25 bc stocksnapper/iStock, p 25 b hrstklnkr/iStock, p 25 bb DeAgostini/Getty Images, p 26 DeA Picture Library/Getty Images, p 27 tl Dennis Steen/Shutterstock, p 27 tr Elena Dijour/Shutterstock, p 27 bl Kiev.Victor/Shutterstock, p 27 br Zherui WU/Shutterstock, p 30 tlorna/Shutterstock, p 31 t GLYN KIRK/AFP/Getty Images, p 31 b MARTIN BUREAU/AFP/Getty Images, p 33 l RetroAtelier/iStock, p 33 r ClassicStock/Alamy, p 37 tr Andresr/Shutterstock, p 37 bl Nataliya_Ostapenko, p 40 Alexander Image/ Shutterstock, p 43 br Lisa S./Shutterstock, p 47 joyfull/Shutterstock, p 48 tl Stanislav Fosenbauer/Shutterstock, p 48 tc Nazzu/Shutterstock, p 48 tr James Jones Jr/Shutterstock, p 48 bl Juraj Kovac/Shutterstock, p 48 bc holbox/Shutterstock, p 48 br totojang1977/Shutterstock, p 50 tl LeonP/Shutterstock, p 50 br Bidagentur Zoonar GmbH/Shutterstock, p 51 tl Chayatorn Laorattanavech/Shutterstock, p 51 tc marco mayer/Shutterstock, p 51 tr Gumenyuk Dmitriy/Shutterstock, p 51 rr wavebreakmedia/Shutterstock, p 51 bl Mega Pixel/Shutterstock, p 51 bc MNI/Shutterstock, p 51 br assistant/Shutterstock, p 52 Michael Buck/Newsteam, p 53 Will Giles/ Getty Images, p 55 tl La Ligue contre le cancer, p 55 bl Amnesty International, p 55 tc Action contre la Faim, p 55 bc Les Amis de la Terre, p 55 tr Médecins Sans Frontières, p 55 br L'UNICEF, p 61 Catalin Petolea/Shutterstock, p 65 Veniamin Kraskov/Shutterstock, p 67 tt Dziewul/Shutterstock, p 67 t Monkey Business Images/Shutterstock, p 67 tc Anna Tyurina/Shutterstock, p 67 bc Piotr Wawrzyniuk/Shutterstock, p 67 b Peter Gudella/Shutterstock, p 67 bb Pinkcandy/Shutterstock, p 68 Cheryl Savan/Shutterstock, p 70 JJ pixs/Shutterstock, p 71 Robert Kneschke/Shutterstock, p 73 Webitect/Shutterstock, p 76 Stefano Cavoretto/Shutterstock, p 77 l Leah-Anne Thompson/Shutterstock, p 77 c RimDream/Shutterstock, p 77r Sapsiwai/Shutterstock, p 85 michaeljung/Shutterstock, p 86 Paul Garnier Rimolo/Shutterstock, p 88 DeAgostini/Getty Images, p 93 Martin Good/Shutterstock, p 94 WireImage/Getty Images.

Mon autoportrait

Draw your self-portrait and complete the sentences below.

Je m'appelle ____.

Ma classe est ____.

Tableau des contenus

Module 1 Questions d'ados

Module 2 Qu'est-ce qui s'est passé?

Module 3 En avant

Module 4 Nos choix

Module 5 Espace culturel

Notes

Exercise Key

reading · writing · listening · speaking · translation

1 Topic 1 Nous sommes tous intelligents

- Pupil Book pages 8–9

Aujourd' hui est ______________________. Il est  ______________.

Langue et grammaire

Present tense

The infinitive is the form of the verb you find in the dictionary. You already know that there are three possible endings: *–er*, *–ir* or *–re*. Here is a reminder of what regular *–er* verbs plus irregular verbs *avoir*, *être*, *faire* and *prendre* look like in the present tense.

	regular –*er*	**avoir**	**être**	**faire**	**prendre**
je/j'	parle	ai	suis	fais	prends
tu	parles	as	es	fais	prends
il/elle/on	parle	a	est	fait	prend
nous	parlons	avons	sommes	faisons	prenons
vous	parlez	avez	êtes	faites	prenez
ils/elles	parlent	ont	sont	font	prennent

Irregular adjectives

Remember that French adjectives agree with the noun they go with. You usually add an *–e* for feminine nouns and an *–s* for plural nouns. However, here are some exceptions.

masculine singular	**masculine plural**	**feminine singular**	**feminine plural**
bon	bons	bonne	bonnes
généreux	généreux	généreuse	généreuses
étranger	étrangers	étrangère	étrangères
actif	actifs	active	actives

Draw lines to link the French and English infinitives.

être | chanter | comprendre | parler | avoir | jouer | écrire

to play | to write | to have | to understand | to be | to speak | to sing

Copy in the appropriate infinitive for each sentence.

avoir | être | parler | chanter
jouer | écrire | comprendre

Être intelligent, c'est…

a bien ________ au tennis.

b ________ des poèmes d'amour.

c ________ quand un ami a un problème.

d ________ comme Madonna.

e ________ fort en physique.

f ________ de bonnes notes au collège.

g ________ anglais, allemand et espagnol.

3 Identify the infinitive of the verb in each of these sentences and write it in.

a Je suis anglais — Infinitive: être

b Nous prenons un coca. — Infinitive: ________

c Tu parles français? — Infinitive: ________

d Qu'est-ce qu'il fait? — Infinitive: ________

e J'ai beaucoup de copains. — Infinitive: ________

f Elle ne comprend pas. — Infinitive: ________

g Ils préparent des crêpes. — Infinitive: ________

h On écrit un e-mail. — Infinitive: ________

4 Use the adjectives to help you work out whether the person being spoken to is male (M) or female (F).

a Tu es généreux. ☐ b Tu es organisée. ☐

c Tu es sportive. ☐ d Tu es généreuse. ☐

e Tu es active. ☐ f Tu es intelligent. ☐

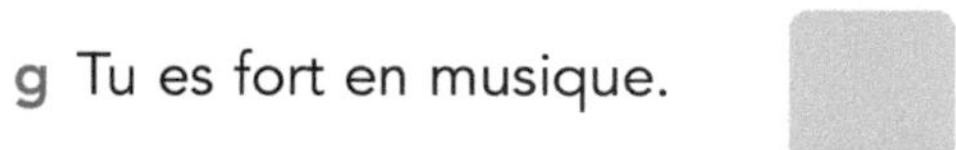

g Tu es fort en musique. ☐ h Tu es forte en maths. ☐

5 Describe these pictures, starting *Il est…* or *Elle est…*

a 

____

b 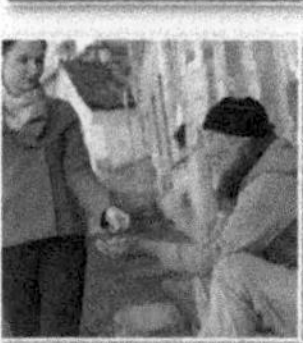

____

c 

____

d 

____

6 In pairs, discuss what you think being intelligent means. The box below contains some infinitives to help you.

jouer chercher avoir être comprendre écrire parler

Exemple

A Pour moi, être intelligent, c'est…

B Ah, bon? Pour moi, être intelligent, c'est…

7 Write T (true) or F (false). ★

Être intelligent: qu'est-ce que c'est?

Tu trouves les maths difficiles? Tu as des problèmes à l'école? Ça ne veut pas dire que tu n'est pas intelligent(e). Tu es peut-être sportif(–ive) ou tu chantes bien? Voilà, c'est une différente sorte d'intelligence.
Une personne aim écouter de la musique, une autre personne aime écrire des blogs ou lire des romans. Toutes ces personnes sont intelligentes!

According to the article…

a If you're no good at school, you can't be intelligent. ________

b A person who is good at singing is intelligent. ________

c A sporty person is intelligent. ________

d People who listen to music are stupid. ________

e Only people who read and write well can be described as intelligent. ________

f There are lots of different types of intelligence. ________

8 Translate these expressions into French using the appropriate infinitives. ★

a being good at maths ________________________

b speaking French ________________________

c understanding problems ________________________

d having good marks ________________________

e writing poems ________________________

f playing football well ________________________

Topic 2 Apprendre une langue

- Pupil Book pages 10–11

Aujourd' hui est  ______________________. Il est  ______________.

Langue et grammaire

Pouvoir, vouloir* and *devoir

Here is a reminder of the different forms of *pouvoir* (to be able to), *vouloir* (to want) and *devoir* (to have to) in the present tense.

	pouvoir	**vouloir**	**devoir**
je	peux	veux	dois
tu	peux	veux	dois
il/elle/on	peut	veut	doit
nous	pouvons	voulons	devons
vous	pouvez	voulez	devez
ils/elles	peuvent	veulent	doivent

All three verbs are followed by another verb in the infinitive.

Tu peux regarder des films.	You can watch films.
Elle veut faire des progrès.	She wants to make progress.
Nous devons écouter le prof.	We must listen to the teacher.

Note the meaning of *vouloir* when it's used with *bien*.

Je veux bien écouter.	I am happy to listen.

Write in the correct form of *vouloir*, *pouvoir* or *devoir* in the boxes. What is the mystery word?

a il… (*pouvoir*) — **a** □□□□

b elles… (*devoir*) — **b** □□□□□□□

c vous… (*pouvoir*) — **c** □□□□□□

d je… (*vouloir*) — **d** □□□□

e elle… (*devoir*) — **e** □□□□

f nous… (*vouloir*) — **f** □□□□□□□

g je… (*devoir*) — **g** □□□□

The mystery word is: ______________

Unjumble these sentences about learning languages. Each one uses *pouvoir*, *vouloir* or *devoir* in the present tense and an infinitive.

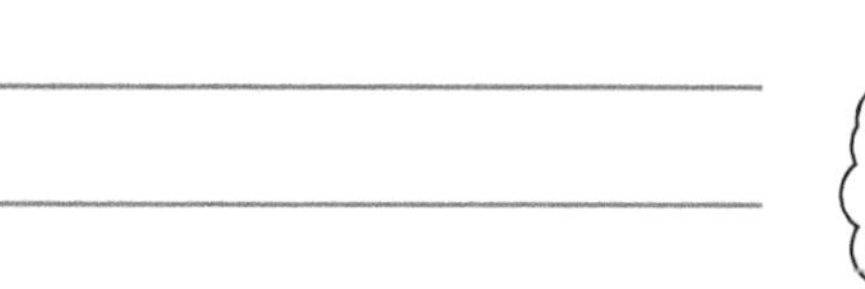

a radio. la Tu écouter peux ______________

b peut lettres. des On écrire ______________

c magazines. Tu lire dois des ______________

d doit la apprendre On grammaire. ______________

e avec Nous un parler devons partenaire. ______________

f MP3. Vous écouter devez des ______________

g le On professeur. écouter doit ______________

h regarder Je des veux DVD. ______________

In pairs. Using vocabulary learned in this module, have a conversation with your partner about what you **must do** and **can do** to learn a language. Each partner should say at least three things.

Exemple

A On peut...

B Oui, et on doit aussi...

Read this article and copy out all the infinitives in the order in which you find them. There are eighteen including the heading. (Some are used several times.)

Apprendre une langue

Aujourd'hui, il est très important d'apprendre une langue étrangère. On doit lire un journal, écouter des conversations, parler avec des collègues et écrire des e-mails. Mais comment apprendre une langue? Ce n'est pas facile. On doit apprendre les mots, comprendre la grammaire, écouter le prof, parler avec des amis et lire des livres. Mais apprendre une langue peut être amusant aussi. On peut discuter en ligne, écouter la radio, regarder des films et écrire des blogs. Allez, bonne chance!

___

___

___

Now re-read the article. Are these things mentioned or not? Put a tick if they are mentioned and a cross if they aren't.

a translating texts ______

b understanding grammar ______

c writing essays ______

d talking to colleagues ______

e watching films ______

f phoning foreign friends ______

g reading magazines ______

h writing out vocabulary ______

6 Find the French for these expressions in exercise 4 and copy them out.

a It's very important to learn a foreign language. ____________________

b You must read a newspaper. ____________________

c You have to understand the grammar. ____________________

d You have to read books. ____________________

e You can have online discussions. ____________________

f You can write blogs. ____________________

g It isn't easy. ____________________

h Good luck! ____________________

7 Answer these questions for yourself using full sentences. ★

a Tu aimes parler français?

Je/J' ____________________

b Tu dois apprendre la grammaire?

____

c Tu peux écrire un blog en français?

____

d Tu dois regarder des DVD?

____

e Tu aimes travailler avec l'ordinateur?

____

f Tu peux comprendre un texte?

____

8 Translate into French. ★

a We must read and write. ____________________

b He must learn the grammar. ____________________

c I want to speak French. ____________________

d You can write to a friend. ____________________

Attention à ton cerveau!

• Pupil Book pages 12–13

Aujourd' hui est  ______________________. Il est  ______________.

Langue et grammaire

The imperative

Remember, you use the imperative when giving advice or instructions.

- Use the singular imperative with people you normally say *tu* to. This is simply the *tu* form of the present tense of a verb without the *tu*. For *–er* verbs, take the letter *s* off the end:
  Mange beaucoup de légumes verts. — Eat lots of green vegetables.
- Use the plural imperative if you are addressing more than one person or someone you normally say *vous* to. This is simply the *vous* form of the verb, without *vous*:
  Pensez à autre chose. — Think about something else.
- Some verbs, such as *être*, have irregular imperatives that you must learn:
  Sois curieux! (singular) — Be curious!
  Soyez curieux! (plural)

Saying 'some' and 'any'

When you want to say 'some' or 'any', use *du*, *de l'*, *de la* or *des*.

masculine	***du** chocolat*
feminine	***de la** salade*
before a vowel (m/f)	***de l'**oxygène*
plural	***des** livres*

Simply use *de* or *d'* after an adverb of quantity or after a negative.

Mange beaucoup de légumes.	Eat lots of vegetables.
Ne prenez pas trop de café.	Don't have too much coffee.
Fais assez d'exercice.	Do enough exercise.
Buvez un peu de jus d'orange.	Drink a little orange juice.

Complete this crossword.

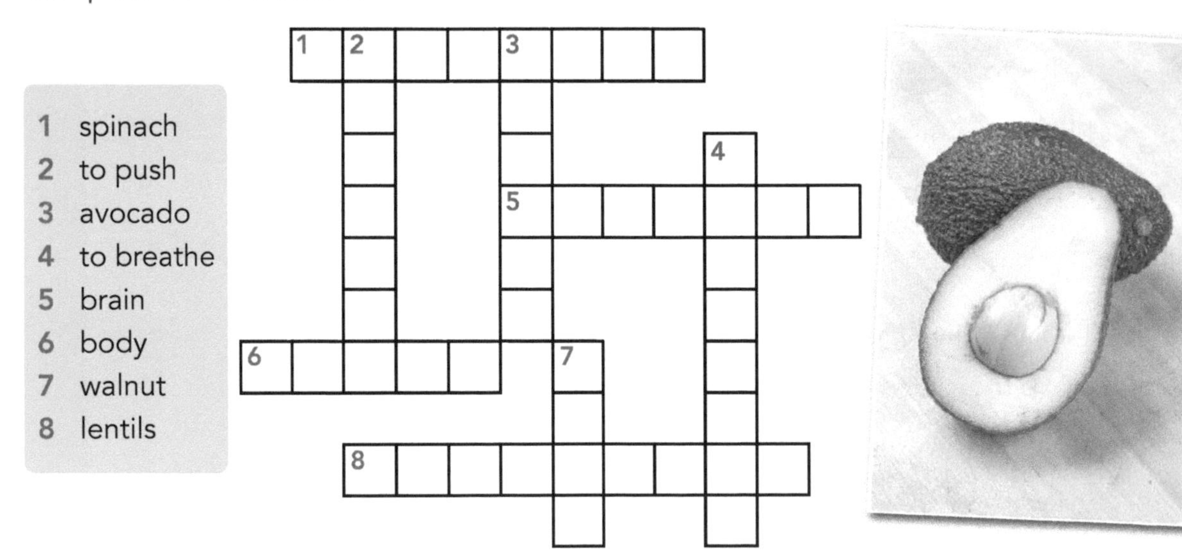

2 Write in *du, de la, de l', des* or *de*.

a beaucoup ________ lait
b ________ épinards
c ________ eau minérale
d ________ salade
e ________ poulet
f ________ viande
g pas ________ chips
h ________ chocolat
i ________ frites
j ________ oxygène
k un peu ________ sucre
l trop ________ limonade

3 Assume that the following sentences are part of a conversation between friends. Is the speaker talking to one person (write 'one') or two people (write 'two')?

a Ne mange pas trop de bonbons. ________

b Buvez beaucoup d'eau. ________

c Soyez prudents. ________

d Fais tes devoirs. ________

e Ne regardez pas trop de télévision. ________

f Prends des légumes. ________

4 Assume that the following sentences are addressed to one person only. Are the sentences in the polite (P) or familiar (F) form?

a Prenez du sucre. ☐
b Mange beaucoup de lentilles. ☐
c Écoute de la musique. ☐
d Ne buvez pas trop de café. ☐
e Lisez le journal. ☐
f Pense toujours à moi! ☐

Read the advice on this website and answer the questions.

soigner = to look after réussir = to succeed

Fais travailler ...

www.ton-cerveau.fr

Fais travailler ton cerveau!

Il faut soigner ton cerveau pour réussir au collège. Lis beaucoup de livres mais ne regarde pas trop de télévision. Mange prudemment, prends beaucoup de légumes (par exemple, des épinards) mais pas trop de viande. Bois surtout du jus de fruit et du lait. Ne prends pas de coca, mais fais un peu de sport tous les jours. Laisse ton portable à la maison et essaie de dormir au moins huit heures par nuit.

a Why is this advice being given? ________________

b What does it say about TV? ________________

c What food is recommended? ________________

d And what drink? ________________

e What does it say about exercise? ________________

f What does it say about mobile phones? ________________

g What should you do for eight hours? ________________

h Is it being addressed to one reader or to several? ________________

6 Translate these instructions into French. ★

a Watch a film (to one person). ________________

b Don't drink wine (to two people). ________________

c Eat some salad (to one person). ________________

d Take a break (to one person). ________________

e Have a walk (to two people). ________________

f Think about your brain (to one person). ________________

7 Translate the text in exercise 5 into English from *Lis beaucoup*... to ...*du lait.* ★

____

____

____

Topic 4 Bien dans ma peau

- Pupil Book pages 14–15

Aujourd' hui est  ______________________. Il est  ______________.

Langue et grammaire

Percentages

The French for percent is *pour cent*:

25%	*vingt-cinq pour cent*
71%	*soixante et onze pour cent*

Comparative adjectives

Remember to use *plus* or *moins* with comparatives:

les cheveux plus courts	shorter hair
les cheveux moins bouclés	less curly hair

Large numbers

Make sure you are comfortable using the following large numbers:

20	*vingt*	70	*soixante-dix*
30	*trente*	80	*quatre-vingts*
40	*quarante*	90	*quatre-vingt-dix*
50	*cinquante*	100	*cent*
60	*soixante*	800	*huit cents*

Copy the correct adjectives under the pictures. Use each adjective twice.

courts longs bouclés raides

a

plus ______________

moins ______________

b

plus ______________

moins ______________

c

plus ______________

moins ______________

d

plus ______________

moins ______________

2 Write these numbers in figures.

a quatre-vingt-cinq ________

b soixante-treize ________

c trois cent quinze ________

d trente-trois ________

e quarante et un ________

f deux cents ________

g cinq cent cinquante ________

h mille neuf cent vingt-deux ________

i quatre-vingt-dix-neuf ________

j soixante et onze ________

3 Read the survey results and write in the percentages in figures.

a ________% don't do any sport.

b ________% have greasy hair.

c ________% have dandruff.

d ________% watch too much TV.

e ________% don't eat well.

f ________% eat too many sweets.

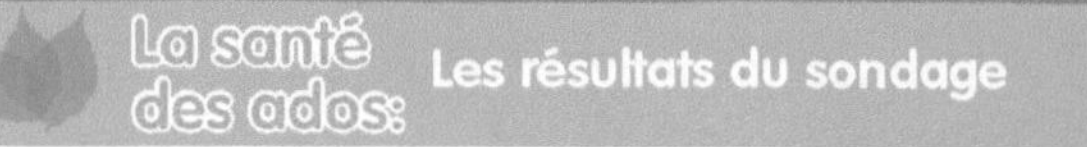

1 Quarante-neuf pour cent des ados ont des pellicules.
2 Trente-huit pour cent des ados mangent trop de bonbons.
3 Soixante-quinze pour cent des ados ont les cheveux gras.
4 Vingt-cinq pour cent des ados ne mangent pas bien.
5 Quatre-vingt-deux pour cent des ados regardent trop la télévision.
6 Dix-huit pour cent des ados ne font pas de sport.

4 Work in pairs. Each partner writes down eight numbers between 20 and 5000. Take turns to read out a number – just once – for your partner to write down.

5 Read the advert. Are the sentences at the top of page 17 true (T) or false (F)?

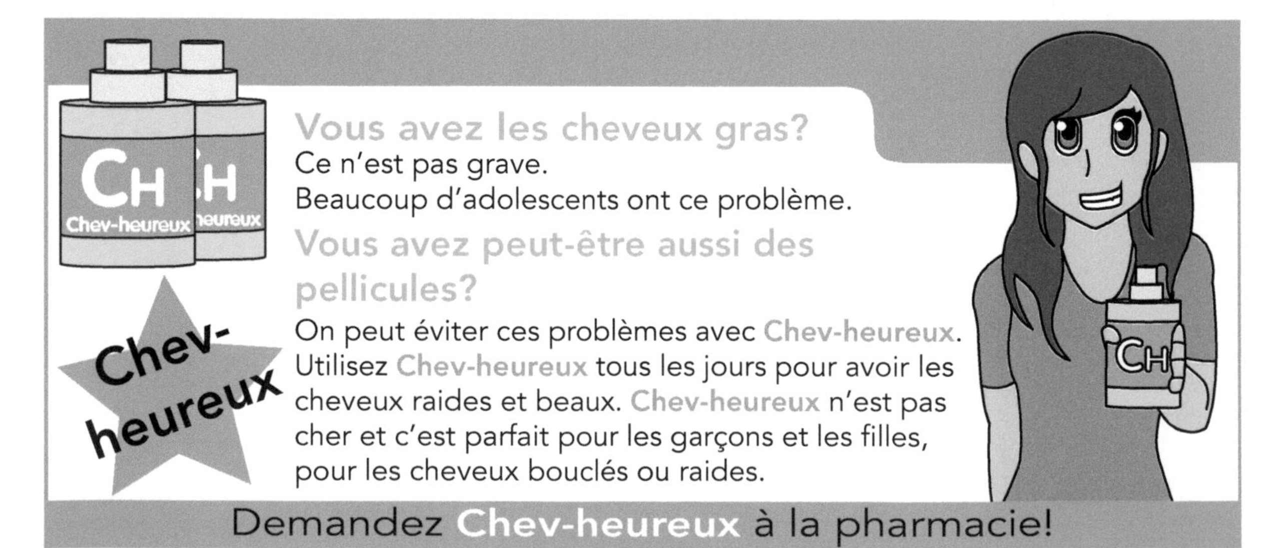

a Chev-heureux is good for greasy hair.

b It isn't suitable for curly hair.

c It's only aimed at girls.

d It won't sort out dandruff.

e It claims to make your hair beautiful.

f It's expensive.

g You can get it in a pharmacy.

h You should use it every day.

6 When you have completed exercise 5, find the sentences in the text that give you the answers and copy them out. Sometimes it may be more than one sentence.

1 *Vous avez les cheveux gras? Ce n'est pas grave.*

2 ______

3 ______

4 ______

5 ______

6 ______

7 ______

7 Translate this text into English.

Un sondage réalisé avec mille ados canadiens a trouvé que:

- 32 pour cent sont mal dans leur peau.
- 83 pour cent parlent facilement avec leurs parents.
- 71 pour cent sont souvent sous pression.
- 66 pour cent se sentent bien à l'école.

8 Refer back to the article in exercise 3 and do some maths. Fill in the blanks with the percentages you have worked out. Write them out in words.

a ______ pour cent mangent bien.

b ______ pour cent n'ont pas les cheveux gras.

c ______ pour cent ne regardent pas trop de télé.

d ______ pour cent font du sport.

e ______ pour cent n'ont pas de pellicules.

f ______ pour cent ne mangent pas trop de bonbons.

Topic 5 La timidité

• Pupil Book pages 16–17

Aujourd' hui est  ______________________________. Il est  ____________________.

Langue et grammaire

Expressions of time

When using expressions of time, pay attention to the word order:

jamais	never
rarement	rarely
quelquefois	sometimes
souvent	often
toujours	always
la plupart du temps	most of the time

Je ne parle jamais en classe.	I never speak in class.
Elle répond rarement aux questions.	She rarely answers questions.
Il travaille toujours dur.	He always works hard.
Tu rougis souvent!	You often blush!

It is also possible to place *quelquefois, souvent, and la plupart du temps* at the very beginning of the sentence.

La plupart du temps, j'ai les mains qui tremblent.	Most of the time, I have shaky hands.
Quelquefois, j'oublie tout!	Sometimes I forget everything!

Copy the correct caption under each picture.

On ne dort pas bien	On transpire	On rougit
Le cœur bat très fort	On tremble	On a mal au ventre

a 

____

b 

____

c 

____

d 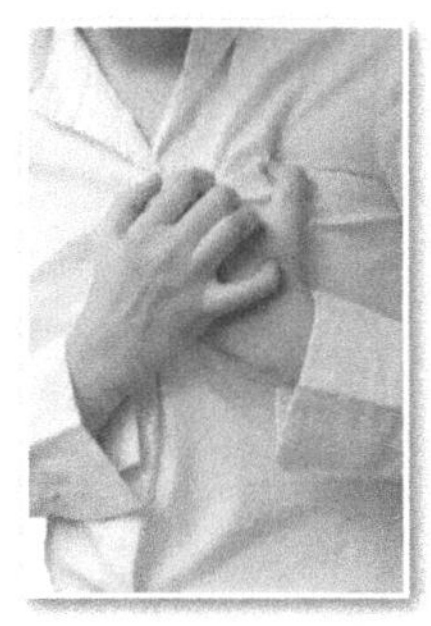

____

e 

____

f 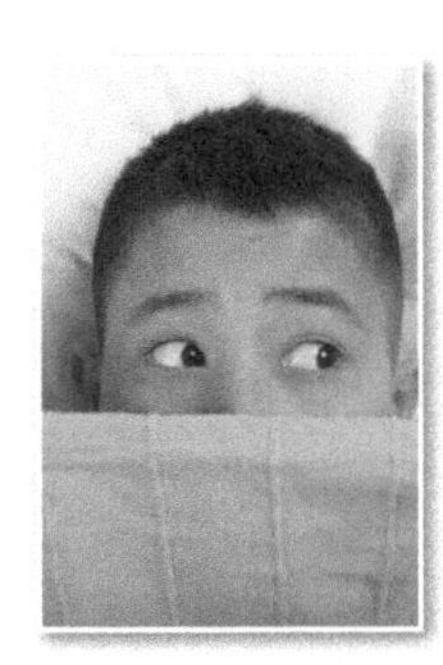

____

2 These words are backwards. Write them out correctly and add the English meanings

	Word	Meaning
a RERIPSNART	________	________
b ERTTAB	________	________
c EDIMIT	________	________
d RELBMERT	________	________
e RUŒC	________	________
f RIGUOR	________	________

3 Write in the French words for these expressions of time.

a often ________

b rarely ________

c always ________

d sometimes ________

e most of the time ________

f never ________

4 Write out these jumbled sentences correctly. Sometimes the expression of time comes at the start of the sentence. Use the capital letters as clues.

a en ne Je jamais parle classe. ________

b toujours fait Abdou exposé. tremble un il quand ________

c mal Quelquefois ventre. au j'ai ________

d timide. Sophie rarement est ________

e temps transpire. plupart je La du ________

f souvent parler. a On de peur ________

5 With a partner, have some fun taking turns to mime symptoms of nervousness.

Exemple

B mimes having terrible stomach ache.

A Tu as mal au ventre?

B Oui!

Read the text and write T (true), F (false) or NM (not mentioned).

a He has stomach ache.

b He feels sick.

c He gets sweaty hands.

d He blushes.

e He feels better afterwards.

f He gets sweaty.

g He gets short of breath.

h His heart beats like a drum.

Write a short account of how you feel before a presentation, an exam or a race. If you're a calm type, use *ne … pas* and *ne … jamais*. ★

____

____

Translate these sentences into French. Pay attention to where you put any expressions of time. ★

a Maeva never blushes. ______________

b Most of the time, I am calm. ______________

c My heart beats fast. ______________

d Lucas rarely has sweaty hands. ______________

e I often tremble and I sometimes sweat. ______________

f I always have stomach ache. ______________

Topic 6 Content de ton look?

- Pupil Book pages 18–19

Aujourd' hui est  ______________________. Il est  ______________.

Langue et grammaire

Demonstrative adjectives

French doesn't usually distinguish between 'this' and 'that', or 'these' and 'those'. However, you do need to use a different word depending on whether the object that you are referring to is masculine or feminine, singular or plural.

masc. singular	***ce*** *problème*	this/that problem
masc. singular (before a vowel)	***cet*** *ami*	this/that friend
fem. singular	***cette*** *question*	this/that question
plural	***ces*** *amis*	these/those friends

Comparatives and superlatives

Remember to use *plus … que* and *moins … que* to make comparisons.

Kimi est ***plus*** *petit* ***que*** *Maeva.*	Kimi is smaller than Maeva.
Zoé est ***moins*** *grande* ***que*** *Chloé.*	Zoé is less tall than Chloé.

When using superlatives, choose the right article: masculine or feminine, singular or plural.

Je suis ***le plus petit.***	I am the smallest.
Elle est ***la plus marrante.***	She is the most fun.
Il a choisi les lunettes ***les plus chères.***	He chose the most expensive glasses.

1 Find the words in the box below to describe these pictures and copy them in.

des lunettes · une voix aigüe · des lentilles · les dents · un appareil dentaire · myope · des boutons · le sourire

a 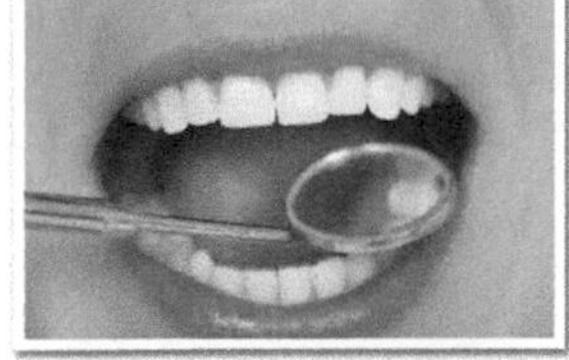 ______________

b 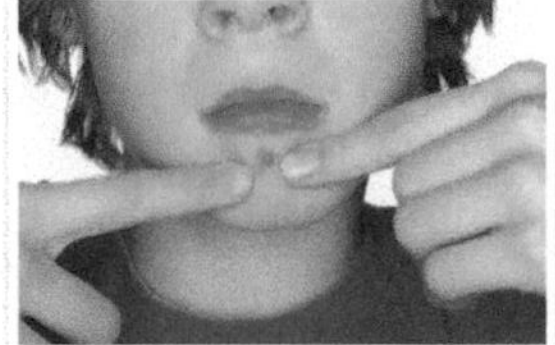 ______________

c  ______________

d 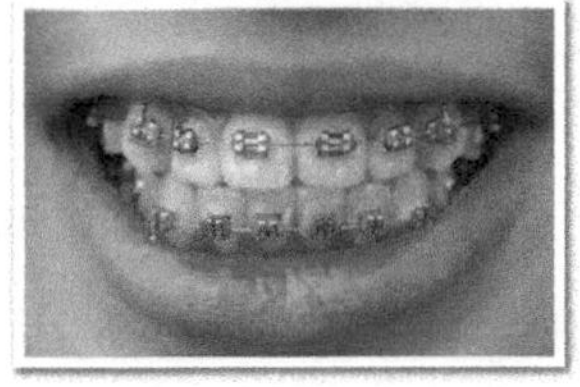 ______________

e 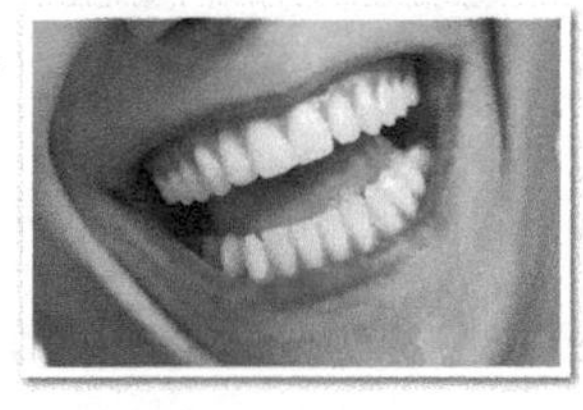 ______________

f 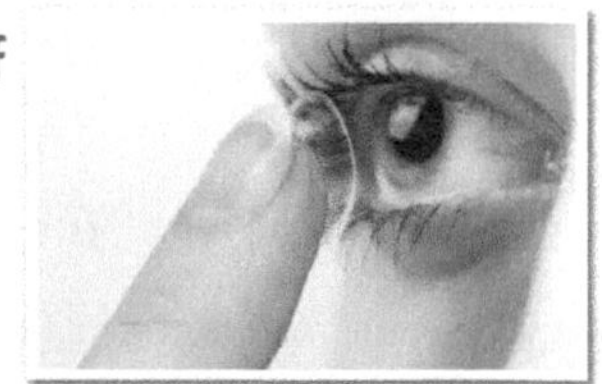 ______________

2 There are lots of negative-sounding expressions in this topic. Translate them into English.

a un inconvénient ______________

b énervant ______________

c désespérant ______________

d aigu ______________

e contraignant ______________

f J'en ai marre! ______________

Under each picture, write an adjective with either *plus* or *moins*.

rapide   cher   difficile   grand   fragile   sympa

a

__________ __________

b

__________ __________

c

__________ __________

d $3^3 \times 5^2 \div 12 - 7^2$ $2 + 2$

__________ __________

e

__________ __________

f

__________ __________

Write in *ce, cet, cette* or *ces.* The genders are provided below.

masculine: article livre ordinateur problème chien appareil élève
feminine: actrice maison chemise photo question lunettes lentilles élève

a ________ problème   b ________ lunettes   c ________ question

d ________ livre   e ________ photo   f ________ article

g ________ actrice   h ________ ordinateur   i ________ appareil

j ________ élèves   k ________ chien   l ________ lentilles

m ________ maison   n ________ chemise

Work in pairs. Draw some contrasting pictures like the ones in exercise 3 to challenge your partner. Take turns to describe what your partner has drawn: *Ce/Cet/Cette … est plus/moins … que ce/cet/cette …* Remember to make the adjective agree with the first noun!

Read the letter and the reply. Choose the right option to complete each sentence below.

Chère Tante Sylvie

Chère Tante Sylvie,
J'ai plusieurs problèmes. Les garçons ne s'intéressent pas à moi parce que je porte des lunettes. J'ai un problème d'acné aussi, et j'en ai marre. Mais le plus grand inconvénient, c'est mon appareil dentaire. Il est en métal et je trouve ça contraignant. Qu'est-ce que je peux faire? Tami

Chère Tami,
Un garçon qui pense que ton apparence est plus importante que ton caractère est un garçon stupide! Mais tu peux faire quelque chose pour tes problèmes. Pour tes boutons, mange moins de bonbons et plus de vitamines. Tu peux aussi essayer des lentilles pour tes yeux et un appareil dentaire avec des élastiques. C'est bon pour les dents et c'est plus chic aussi. Tante Sylvie

a Tami wears glasses/contact lenses.

b Her skin is perfect/spotty.

c She likes/dislikes her dental brace.

d Her dental brace is her biggest/smallest problem.

e She finds it easy/hard to get boyfriends.

f She can do something/nothing about her problems.

g A brace with elastics is cool/embarrassing.

h Boys who put appearance first are sensible/stupid.

7 Translate Tami's letter in exercise 6 into English from *Les garçons…* to *…contraignant.* ★

Write five sentences saying 'This … is more/less … than that …' Here are some adjectives to give you ideas.

marrant moche pratique sympa compliqué difficile facile joli

Ce tee-shirt est moins cher que ce pantalon.

2 Topic 1 Les stars de l'histoire

- Pupil Book pages 32–33

Aujourd' hui est  ________________________ . Il est  ________________ .

Langue et grammaire.

Using *est-ce que* to form questions

You can use the structure *est-ce que* to form a number of different questions. Use a question word in front of it, like this:

Où est-ce que tu es allé?	Where did you go?
Quand est-ce que tu es allé?	When did you go?
Pourquoi est-ce que tu es allé?	Why did you go?
Qui est-ce que tu préfères?	Who do you prefer?

Another very useful question you can use is:
Qu'est-ce qui s'est passé? What happened?

Saying dates

Remember that the usual way of saying a year in French is different from the way it is said in English:

1964	*mille neuf cent soixante-quatre*
2002	*deux mille deux*

Fill in the grid. Many of the French words are similar to the English words but not exactly the same so be careful with your spelling!

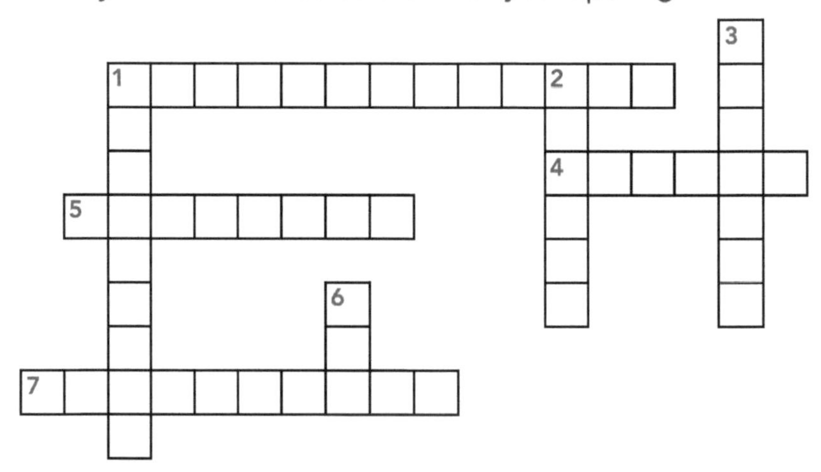

Across:
1 demonstration
4 people
5 battle
7 prisoner

Down:
1 monarchy
2 taxes
3 equality
6 king

Write down the years in numbers.

a mille huit cent trente-trois ________

b mille sept cent soixante-neuf ________

c deux mille quinze ________

d deux mille vingt-deux ________

e mille neuf cent quarante-cinq ________

f mille six cent quatre-vingt-trois ________

3 Now write these dates out in words.

a 1742 ______________________

b 1925 ______________________

c 2006 ______________________

d 1666 ______________________

e 2014 ______________________

f 1815 ______________________

4 Draw lines to link the pictures to the names.

1 

2

3 

4 

5 

6 

a Marie-Antoinette

b Joséphine Bonaparte

c Louis XIV

d Louis XVI

e Napoléon Bonaparte

f Jeanne d'Arc

5 Have a question and answer session with a partner about French history. Take it in turns to ask the questions and answer them with the help of the information below.

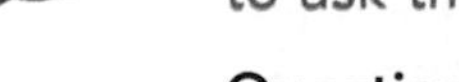

Questions	**Information**
• Qu'est-ce qui s'est passé en 1429?	Napoléon Bonaparte est devenu empereur de la France. (1804)
• Qu'est-ce qui s'est passé en 1643?	Jeanne d'Arc a gagné la Bataille d'Orléans. (1429)
• Qu'est-ce qui s'est passé en 1789?	Louis XIV est devenu roi de France. (1643)
• Qu'est-ce qui s'est passé en 1804?	La Révolution française a commencé. (1789)

Translate these questions into English.

a Qu'est-ce qui s'est passé en 1804?

____

b Quand est-ce que la Révolution française a commencé?

____

c Où est-ce que Jeanne d'Arc a gagné une bataille?

____

d De qui est-ce que Joséphine Bonaparte a divorcé?

____

e Pourquoi est-ce qu'il y a des célébrations le 14 juillet?

____

f Quand est-ce qu'on a libéré la Bastille?

____

7 Write these questions in French, using *est-ce que* and the *tu* form. ★

a What happened? _______________

b Where did you go? _______________

c Why did you go to Paris? _______________

d When did you go to Paris? _______________

e What did you see in Paris? _______________

Read the text and fill in the gaps in the English summary. ★

The French people were _______ and _______. There was no _______ and they had to pay high _______. In 1789, there was a _______ in Paris. The people _______ the prisoners kept in the _______. That was the end of the French _______. Nowadays, France is a _______.

La Révolution française a commencé parce que la plupart du peuple français avait faim et était très pauvre. Il n'y avait pas d'égalité et le peuple n'était pas content parce qu'il devait payer trop d'impôts. En 1789, il y a eu une manifestation à Paris et on a attaqué la Bastille et libéré les prisonniers. C'était la fin pour la monarchie française. Aujourd'hui, la France est une république.

2 Topic 2 On a fêté le 14 juillet

• Pupil Book pages 34–35

Aujourd' hui est  ______________________. Il est  ______________.

Langue et grammaire

The third person in the perfect tense

Remember that the perfect tense is formed using the present tense of the auxiliary verb *avoir* or *être* together with a past participle.

For the third person use:

- *a* (singular) or *ont* (plural) for verbs which take *avoir* as the auxiliary verb.
  For example:

elle a dansé	she danced
il a mangé	he ate
elles ont regardé	they (f) watched
ils ont vu	they (m) saw

- *est* (singular) or *sont* (plural) for verbs which take *être* as the auxiliary verb. Remember that the past participle has to agree for verbs that use *être*:

*elle est allé**e***	she went
il est allé	he went
*elles sont parti**es***	they (f) left
*ils se sont déguisé**s***	they (m) dressed up

Il y a eu

The perfect tense of *il y a* is *il y a eu*. This is used to describe an event which happened in the past. This is different from *il y avait*, which is used to describe a past situation.

Il y a eu un concert. There was a concert.

1 Unjumble the anagrams to find ways of celebrating 14 July and write the French words under the appropriate pictures.

un eiemtng éraien   un cconetr grttuai   un déiélf miitlraie   un fue d'ractifie

a 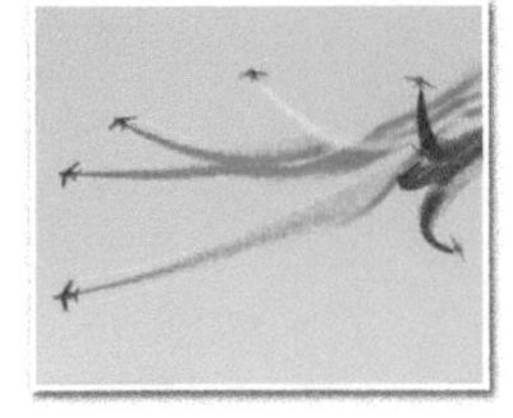

b 

c 

d 

______________ ______________ ______________ ______________

2 Put a tick by any sentence written in the third person. Leave all the others blank.

a Thomas a regardé les avions.  ☐

b Je suis allée à une fête. ☐

c On a célébré le 14 juillet.  ☐

d Nous sommes allés à un bal. ☐

e Je me suis déguisé.  ☐

f Ils ont vu un défilé. 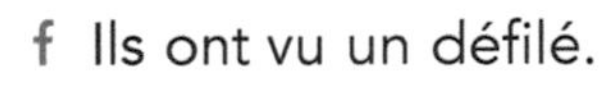 ☐

g As-tu dansé? 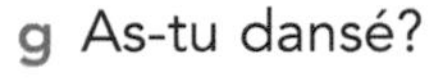  ☐

h On est allé voir un feu d'artifice. ☐

i Elles sont rentrées à minuit.  ☐

j Chloé a écouté de la musique. ☐

3 Complete these sentences with *a*, *est*, *ont* or *sont*.

a On ________ allés à une fête.

b Elle s' ________ déguisée.

c Ils ________ allés à un bal.

d Il ________ allé à un concert gratuit.

e Elle ________ regardé le défilé.

f On ________ écouté de la musique classique.

g Ils se ________ couchés vers onze heures.

h Maeva et Chloé ________ dansé toute la soirée.

4 Find these French expressions in the text and copy them out.

Cette année, comme toujours, on a célébré la fête nationale dans notre village. Il y a eu un défilé sur la place et un feu d'artifice dans le parc. Le soir, il y a eu un bal à l'hôtel de ville. On a dansé et chanté et on s'est amusés.

a in the evening ________

b there was a procession ________

c there was a ball ________

d we had fun ________

e as always ________

f this year ________

5 With a partner, take turns to ask and answer these questions about the text in exercise 4. Try to answer in full sentences.

a Quand est-ce qu'on a célébré la fête nationale?

b Où est-ce qu'il y a eu un défilé?

c Qu'est-ce qu'il y a eu dans le parc?

d Où est-ce qu'il y a eu un bal?

e Qu'est-ce qu'on a fait pendant le bal?

6 Translate the questions in exercise 5 into English.

____

____

____

____

____

7 Translate this passage into English. ★

Pour célébrer le 14 juillet, mon frère a organisé un concert chez nous. Il a passé toute la journée à se préparer. Ses copains ont joué de leurs instruments de musique et mes parents ont préparé à manger: un grand gâteau bleu, blanc et rouge! On s'est vraiment bien amusés.

8 Translate these sentences into French. ★

décorer manger aller se déguiser organiser s'amuser

a My parents organised a party.

b My father decorated the house.

c My sister dressed up.

d My brother ate too much.

e He went to bed at 10 o'clock.

f We (*On*) had fun.

2 Topic 3 Les gros titres de ma vie

• Pupil Book pages 36–37

Aujourd' hui est  ______________________ . Il est  ______________ .

Langue et grammaire

Using the perfect tense with *être*

It is important to remember which verbs use *être* as their auxiliary in the perfect tense. Here is a list:

aller	to go
arriver	to arrive, to happen
descendre	to go down, to get off
entrer	to go in, to come in
monter	to go up, to come up
mourir	to die
naître	to be born
partir	to leave, to go
passer	to pass (by)
rester	to stay
retourner	to return
sortir	to go out
tomber	to fall
venir	to come

Verbs which are based on these verbs also use *être* as the auxiliary.

devenir	to become
revenir	to come back

And don't forget that reflexive verbs also use *être* as the auxiliary.

Je me suis habillé(e).	I got dressed.

Using adjectives

Use *c'était* with interesting adjectives to describe what a situation in the past was like:

En 2000, j'ai participé aux Jeux olympiques. C'était passionnant!	In 2000 I participated in the Olympic Games. It was exciting!
Le voyage a duré 30 heures. C'était épuisant.	The journey took 30 hours. It was exhausting.

1 Which French adjective would you use to describe these feelings?

exigeant gratifiant épuisant stressant exaltant passionnant

a You're on a roller coaster. ______________

b You're climbing a very steep hill on your mountain bike. ______________

c You're freaking out about an exam. ______________

d You're doing charity work and you feel good about it. ______________

e You've finished your mountain bike ride. ______________

f You're thrilled about a concert you're going to. ______________

2 Which of these verbs use *être* in the perfect tense? Write *Ê* (*être*) or *A* (*avoir*).

a venir	b entrer	c voir
d aller	e regarder	f acheter
g rester	h aimer	i commencer
j arriver	k écouter 	l partir
m lire	n participer 	o sortir

3 Read this article and decide whether the sentences about it are true (T) or false (F).

a She was born in the Caribbean.

b She's never played in America.

c She was born in the eighties.

d She's never won at Wimbledon.

e She was beaten by Sabine Lisicki.

f Marion is still playing professionally. 

Je suis née le 2 octobre 1984 à Puy-en-Velay, France. En 2006, je suis partie pour jouer aux États-Unis. En 2013, je suis allée en Angleterre pour participer au tournoi de Wimbledon. Je suis devenue championne en gagnant contre Sabine Lisicki. J'ai eu beaucoup de problèmes avec l'entraînement et je me suis retirée du tennis professionnel en août 2013.

4 In pairs. Do an interview with Marion. A asks the questions and B answers. Be polite and use the vous form in your questions. Then swap roles. Ask:

- where she was born
- when she went to the USA
- when she won Wimbledon
- when she retired.

5 Insert the appropriate time expressions.

__________ (*in the beginning*), Marion n'avait pas de problèmes de forme. Mais elle s'est blessée pendant un tournoi en 2005 et __________ (*from that moment on*), elle a commencé à avoir des difficultés. Elle a joué en Nouvelle-Zélande et __________ (*then*) elle est devenue championne du Japon. __________ (*since*) sa victoire à Wimbledon, elle n'a pas joué, __________ (*so*) elle s'est retirée.

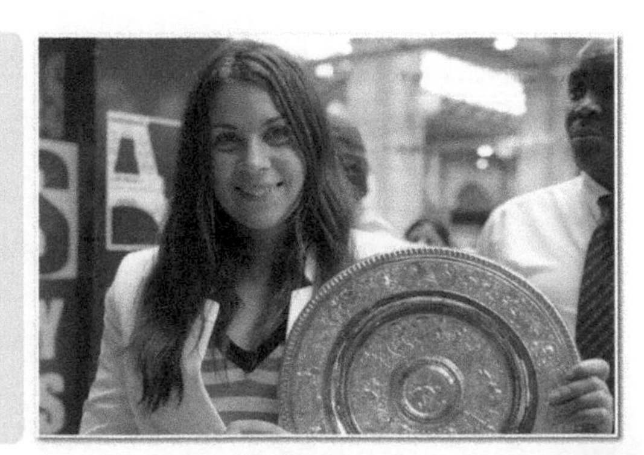

6 Insert the correct part of *être* and the past participle. Pay attention to the gender of the person.

a Emma ______ ______ à minuit. (*came back*)

b Hugo ______ ______ en retard. (*arrived*)

c Zoé ______ ______ à midi. (*departed*)

d Noah ______ ______ après Zoé. (*went out*)

e Sarah ______ ______ championne. (*became*)

f Adam ______ ______. (*got dressed*)

g Lucas et Nathan ______ ______ en 1999. (*were born*)

h Camille et Alice ______ ______ en Autriche. (*went*)

7 Translate the sentences into English.

a C'était stressant parce que je n'avais pas d'argent.

____

b Le concert était passionnant parce que j'adore Lady Gaga.

____

c C'était épuisant parce que j'ai participé à un marathon.

____

d Le film d'amour était émouvant.

____

e C'était gratifiant parce qu'elle a gagné le tournoi.

____

8 Translate into French. ★

a I participated in the Olympic Games.

____

b It was stressful and exhausting.

____

c So I retired in June.

____

d Then I went to America.

____

e From that moment on, I was happier.

____

2 Topic 4 La Belle Époque

- Pupil Book pages 38–39

Aujourd' hui est  ______________________. Il est  ______________.

Langue et grammaire

Imperfect tense

The imperfect tense is often used to describe a routine in the past.

Tous les jours elle se levait à 9h. Every day she used to get up at 9 a.m. / Every day she got up at 9 a.m.

Souvent il arrivait vers 10h. He often used to arrive at about 10 a.m. / He often arrived at about 10 a.m.

Demonstrative pronouns

Demonstrative pronouns are used to refer to a noun which has already been mentioned. In English, we would say 'the one' or 'the ones'. In French, the demonstrative pronoun must agree with the noun it is replacing:

- *celui* (masculine singular)
- *celle* (feminine singular)
- *ceux* (masculine plural)
- *celles* (feminine plural)

*Quel livre veux-tu? **Celui** de gauche coûte 15€ mais **ceux** de droite coûtent 5€.* Which book do you want? The one on the left costs €15 but the ones on the right cost €5.

*Regarde les femmes sur cette photo. **Celle** d'en haut est Mme Choquet et **celles** d'en bas sont ses filles.* Look at the women in this photo. The one at the top is Mme Choquet and the ones at the bottom are her daughters.

1 Fill in the 'Imperfect' column with the imperfect form of these verbs. Remember, to form the imperfect tense, take the stem and add these endings:

	Present	Imperfect	End of sentence (exercise 2)
a	je me lève	Je me levais	à 7h.
b	il regarde		
c	on mange		
d	nous jouons		
e	elle porte		
f	je suis		
g	vous habitez		
h	tu travailles		
i	je visite		
j	on sort		

je	–ais
tu	–ais
il/elle/on	–ait
nous	–ions
vous	–iez
ils/elles	–aient

2 Now fill in the 'End of sentence' column in exercise 2 in any way you like (as long as it makes sense!).

The one on the left or the one on the right? Answer the questions using a word from the box followed by *de gauche* or *de droite*.

celui celle ceux celles

a Quel chapeau est plus grand? ________

b Quelles chaussures sont noires? ________

c Quels cheveux sont blonds? ________

d Quelle femme est plus moderne? ________

e Quelle image préfères-tu? ________

Decide whether these sentences describe a one-off activity or a regular activity in the past. Write 'O' or 'R'.

a Je me levais à 8h. ☐

b Elle s'est levée à 7h. ☐

c On allait dans le sud de la France. ☐

d On est allé en voiture. ☐

e J'ai mangé un œuf. ☐

f Elle mangeait beaucoup de céréales. ☐

g Marion jouait au tennis. ☐

h Nous avons joué au minigolf. ☐

i Je faisais la vaisselle. ☐

j J'ai fait mes devoirs. ☐

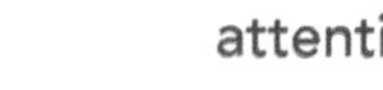

In pairs. Use these pictures for a guessing game. A picks a set, then silently chooses one of the three objects in that set. B guesses which object has been chosen, paying attention to the gender of its name, as given below. Then swap roles.

Exemple

masculine:	livre	croissant	crayon
feminine:	fleur	tasse	chaussette

A Numéro 3.
B C'est celui de gauche?
A Non.
B C'est celui du milieu?
A Oui!

B Numéro 4.
A C'est celle de droite?
B Non.
A C'est celle de gauche?
B Oui!

1 

2 

3 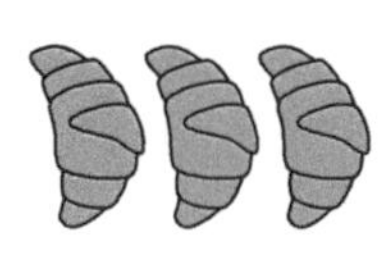

4 

5 

6 

6 Read the text and find these French expressions.

Les années soixante

Moi, j'étais étudiant pendant les années soixante. C'était une époque de changement. Je portais des chemises à fleurs et un pantalon à pattes d'éléphant. C'est gênant! Les filles portaient des jupes longues et des bandeaux. Je me levais à midi et l'après-midi j'écoutais de la musique psychédélique. Le soir, je faisais de la méditation. Je participais à des manifestations politiques et je m'engageais pour la paix.

a a period ______________ b the sixties ______________

c demonstrations ______________ d flared trousers ______________

e peace ______________ f student ______________

7 Write down all the imperfect tense verbs in the text of exercise 6. There are nine to find.

____

____

8 Re-read the exercise 6 text and answer these questions.

a What did he wear? ______________

b How does he feel about that now? ______________

c What did he do in the afternoons? ______________

d And in the evenings? ______________

e What did the girls wear? ______________

9 Write five sentences about things you used to do, using the imperfect tense. They don't have to be true! ★

____

____

____

____

____

2 Topic 5 Quand j'étais petit(e)

• Pupil Book pages 40–41

Aujourd' hui est  ______________________. Il est  ______________.

Langue et grammaire

The imperfect tense

Use the imperfect tense to describe a past situation or something that you used to do. The following endings are added to the stem of the verb:

je	–ais	*nous*	–ions
tu	–ais	*vous*	–iez
il/elle/on	–ait	*ils/elles*	–aient

j'habitais	I lived / I used to live
il habitait	he lived / he used to live
ils/elles habitaient	they lived / they used to live

For *être*, use *ét–* as the stem and then add the imperfect ending.

Negative constructions

ne ... pas	*Je **ne** mange **pas** de viande.*	I don't eat meat.
ne ... jamais	*Tu **ne** joues **jamais** au foot.*	You never play football.
ne ... plus	*Il **n'**habite **plus** à Paris.*	He doesn't live in Paris any more.
ne ... rien	*Elle **ne** veut **rien**.*	She doesn't want anything.
ne ... que	Je **ne** mange **que** des légumes.	I only eat vegetables.

Pronunciation

Except for the *nous* and *vous* forms of the imperfect tense, all the endings are pronounced in exactly the same way. You just need to remember the different spellings when you are writing.

1 Write in an appropriate pronoun to match each of these imperfect verb forms. In many cases more than one pronoun is possible.

a ________ regardais
b ________ jouions
c ________ voulaient
d ________ habitiez
e ________ pouvait
f ________ fermais
g ________ allait
h ________ aviez
i ________ parlions
j ________ existaient

2 Now write in the correct imperfect verb forms.

a je ______________ (*parler*)
b elle ______________ (*vouloir*)
c nous ______________ (*avoir*)
d tu ______________ (*regarder*)
e ils ______________ (*habiter*)
f vous ______________ (*pouvoir*)
g il ______________ (*aller*)
h elles ______________ (*exister*)
i je ______________ (*jouer*)
j nous ______________ (*fermer*)

Identify the negative constructions in these sentences. Write the correct letter next to each sentence.

1 Ma mère ne joue jamais avec l'ordinateur. ______

2 Je ne fume pas. ______

3 Tu ne veux rien manger? ______

4 Paule ne fait plus de sport. ______

5 Nous ne prenons que de la salade, merci. ______

a never doing something

b not doing something any more

c only doing something

d not doing something

e not doing anything

In pairs. A chooses five things that he or she does. B says that he/she **never** does those things, using *ne … jamais*. Then swap roles.

Exemple

A Je regarde la télé tous les jours.

B C'est vrai? Moi, je ne regarde jamais la télé.

Read the text and copy out all the imperfect verbs. There are fifteen (including repeats).

Quand j'ai commencé l'école primaire j'aimais beaucoup le prof. M. Lemont était très gentil. Nous jouions pendant la récré mais nous travaillions aussi. J'avais beaucoup de copains mais j'étais très naïf! Je croyais qu'il était possible d'amener mon chien à l'école! M. Lemont n'était pas content. Je pensais aussi qu'on pouvait manger pendant les cours. Et je croyais qu'on pouvait rentrer à la maison avant la fin des cours. Pendant deux semaines, je quittais l'école à 11 heures et je rentrais chez moi! M. Lemont a téléphoné à ma mère.

____

____

____

____

6 Find and copy out the two sentences that use the perfect tense.

7 Explain why this text is written mainly in the imperfect tense. Explain also why two of the sentences are in the perfect.

8 Translate the text into English from '*M. Lemont n'était pas content…*' to the end. ★

9 Translate these sentences into French. Four use the imperfect tense, one uses the present tense and four use a negative construction. ★

a I used to go to school by bike.

b We never used to play handball.

c They didn't used to like vegetables.

d We don't eat vegetables any more.

e I only used to speak English.

Mai '68

• Pupil Book pages 42–43

Aujourd' hui est  ______________________. Il est  ______________.

Langue et grammaire

Using the perfect and imperfect tenses together
When you're telling a story it's useful to be able to use both the perfect and the imperfect tenses. You have seen how to use the imperfect tense to describe a routine in the past. You can also use the imperfect tense to describe the situation or the background to a story. Use the perfect tense to talk about the events that took place in the past.

Look at the examples of these two tenses being used together:

J'habitais à Paris quand j'ai rencontré Léa. — I was living in Paris when I met Léa.
Il rentrait à la maison quand il a vu l'accident. — He was going home when he saw the accident.

1 Read the sentences a–h. Write 'imperfect' or 'perfect' next to the activities 1–16 below.

a J'habitais à Rouen quand j'ai rencontré ma femme.
b Je conduisais une voiture quand j'ai vu un renard.
c Pendant que nous mangions, le téléphone a sonné.
d Pendant que je travaillais, j'ai mangé un croissant.
e Il allait en ville quand il a vu l'accident.
f Pendant que Sophie faisait ses devoirs, Abdou a joué avec son portable.
g Pendant que nous faisions un pique-nique, un chien a mangé nos sandwichs.
h Le prof parlait quand le directeur est entré.

1 having a picnic ______________
2 working ______________
3 the head teacher entering ______________
4 the phone ringing ______________
5 eating ______________
6 driving a car ______________
7 meeting my wife ______________
8 the teacher talking ______________
9 going into town ______________
10 living in Rouen ______________
11 seeing an accident ______________
12 playing with a mobile phone ______________
13 eating a croissant ______________
14 a dog eating sandwiches ______________
15 doing homework ______________
16 seeing a fox ______________

2 Write in the appropriate imperfect tense verbs.

habitaient était étais étaient voulaient travaillaient luttaient aimaient

a J'________ à Paris.

b Les étudiants ________ plus de liberté.

c C'________ dangereux.

d Les jeunes ne ________ pas.

e Ils n'________ pas la police.

f Les rues ________ dangereuses.

g Les étudiants ________ contre la police.

h Quatre personnes ________ dans un appartement.

In pairs. Have a conversation about one-off things you did on holiday.

Exemple

A Quand j'étais en vacances, j'ai nagé dans la mer.

B Et moi, quand j'étais en vacances, j'ai eu un accident.

4 Read the text and find the French for the items of vocabulary listed below.

En 2005, j'avais 15 ans. J'habitais avec ma famille dans un petit appartement dans un immeuble à Clichy-sous-Bois, dans la banlieue de Paris. Je sortais souvent le soir pour jouer au football dans la rue. Mais le 27 octobre, je suis resté à la maison. Pourquoi? Parce qu'il y avait des problèmes dans les rues de la cité. Jeudi 27 octobre, à 17h20, plusieurs agents de police sont arrivés pour faire une enquête sur un crime. Deux adolescents innocents, Zyed Benna et Bouna Traoré, ont essayé d'échapper aux policiers en se cachant dans un transformateur électrique. Les deux garçons ont été électrocutés dans un accident tragique.

À cause de ça, des affrontements entre la police et les jeunes ont commencé dans la région parisienne. Presque 9000 voitures et des douzaines d'écoles ont été détruites et beaucoup de jeunes gens, policiers et pompiers ont été blessés. Les troubles ont duré plusieurs semaines. Environ 2900 manifestants ont été arrêtés.

a demonstrators ________________ b killed ________________

c to escape ________________ d suburb ________________

e dozens ________________ f destroyed ________________

g injured ________________ h to investigate ________________

i high-rise building ________________ j clashes ________________

5 Explain why the first few sentences of the exercise 4 text use the imperfect tense and the rest uses the perfect.

6 Answer these questions.

a What did Pascal normally do in the evenings?

b What did he do on 27 October 2005?

c Why?

d Why did the police arrive at Clichy-sous-Bois?

e Where did the two youngsters hide?

f What happened in Paris as a result of the incident?

7 Translate the last paragraph of the text in question 4 into English.

8 Translate into French.

a I was working at home when the phone rang.

b We were watching TV when the dog ate my cake.

c Mouna was in the street when she saw the accident.

3 Topic 1 Sept milliards d'habitants

• Pupil Book pages 56–57

Aujourd' hui est  ______________________. Il est  ______________.

Langue et grammaire

High numbers

1 000	*mille*
2 000	*deux mille*
1 000 000	*un million*
2 000 000	*deux millions*
1 000 000 000	*un milliard*

Use *de* or *d'* to introduce a noun after *million(s)* and *milliard(s)*, but not after *mille.*

deux cent mille habitants	200 000 inhabitants
trois millions de personnes	3 000 000 people
sept milliards d'habitants.	7 000 000 000 inhabitants

Milliardième

Remember that to create an ordinal number, you simply add *–ième* at the end of the required number:

troisième	third
millionième	millionth
milliardième	billionth

For numbers ending in *e*, remember to drop the e before you add *–ième*:

quatrième fourth *millième* thousandth

Plus and *moins*

Use *le/la plus* with an adjective to mean 'the most':

le plus grand	the largest
la plus peuplée	the most populated

You can also use it with *de* and a noun:

le plus de pesticides the most pesticides

Use *plus de* or *moins de* with a number to say 'more than' or 'less than':

Elle a moins de 15 ans. She is less than 15 years old.

Pronunciation

Remember that letters of the alphabet are pronounced differently in French. Listen to how ONU and CO_2 are spoken.

Write in the population of each country in numbers.

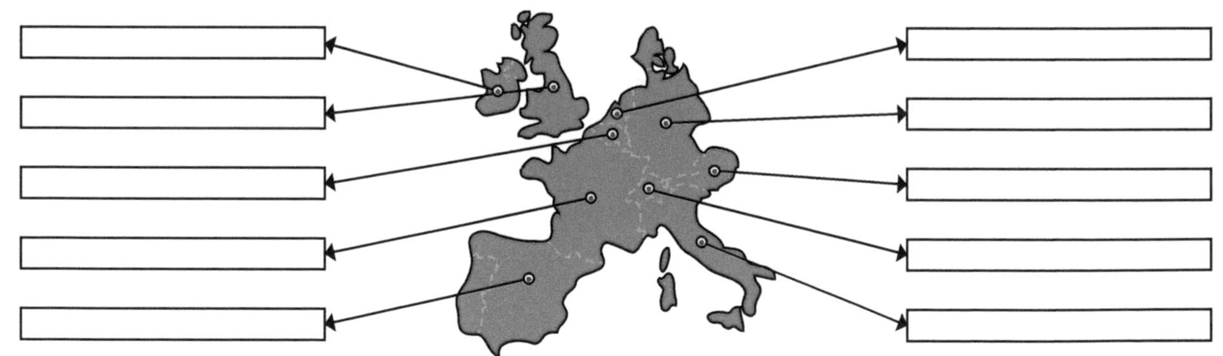

- La France a soixante-six millions d'habitants.
- La Belgique a onze millions d'habitants.
- Le Royaume-Uni a soixante-trois millions d'habitants.
- L'Allemagne a quatre-vingt-deux millions d'habitants.
- L'Espagne a quarante-sept millions d'habitants.
- L'Italie a soixante et un millions d'habitants.
- La Suisse a huit millions d'habitants.
- Les Pays-Bas ont dix-sept millions d'habitants.
- L'Autriche a neuf millions d'habitants.
- L'Irlande a cinq millions d'habitants.

2 Translate into French and fill in the country names.

a The most populous country is _______.   b The least populous country is _______.

_______________________________   _______________________________

3 Fill in the league table of European countries by size of population. Also write in *le premier pays, le deuxième pays,* etc.

	Les populations des pays d'Europe		
1	l'Allemagne	82 millions	le premier pays
2			
3			
4			
5			
6			
7			
8			
9			
10			

4 In pairs. A spells the names of these organisations out loud in French. B (without looking) writes down the words. Then swap roles.

a UNESCO

b Greenpeace

c Amnesty International

d UNICEF

e Emmaüs

f l'Arche de Zoé

g Médecins sans frontières

h Comité international pour la protection des droits de l'homme

5 Round the numbers up or down to the nearest million (a–f) or the nearest ten thousand (g–j) and write them out in words.

Émissions de CO_2 (milliers de tonnes)

a	Chine	7 031 916	sept millions
b	États-Unis	5 461 014	
c	Union européenne	4 177 817	
d	Inde	1 742 698	
e	Russie	1 708 653	
f	Japon	1 208 163	
g	Allemagne	786 660	
h	Canada	544 091	
i	Iran	538 404	
j	Royaume-Uni	522 856	

Answer these questions.

a How many people are there in the world?

____

b What does that cause?

____

c What does the text say about a billion people?

____

d And what does it say about 870 million?

____

e Why is China mentioned?

____

f Why exactly is France mentioned?

____

Translate these phrases into French.

a the most pesticides ______________

b the youngest country ______________

c the oldest country ______________

d twenty billion ______________

e the five millionth person ______________

f the five billionth person ______________

Topic 2 La ville de demain

• Pupil Book pages 58–59

Aujourd' hui est ______________________. Il est ______________.

Langue et grammaire

The future tense

This topic uses the future tense with the third person singular (*il/elle/on*) and plural (*ils/elles*). To make the future tense of regular *–er* verbs, simply take the verb in the infinitive and add *–a* in the singular and *–ont* in the plural:

habiter	*Elle habitera en ville.*	She'll live in town.
cultiver	*On cultivera des légumes.*	We'll grow vegetables.
recycler	*Ils recycleront l'eau.*	They'll recycle water.

For all other verbs, the same endings apply, but you need to learn the stem used to make the future tense. Remember that the stem used to make the future tense always ends in *–r*.

The future stem of *être* (to be) is *ser–*. The future stem of *avoir* (to have) is *aur–*.

La ville sera verte. The city will be green. *Il y aura beaucoup d'arbres.* There will be many trees.

Opinions

When introducing an opinion with phrases such as *je pense*, remember to include the word *que*.

Je crois que tu es trop pessimiste. I think that you are too pessimistic.

You can also use the phrase *à mon avis*.

À mon avis, ce sera fantastique. In my opinion, it will be fantastic.

Solve the picture clues. What is the mystery word in the tinted boxes (down) and what does it mean?

1 ☐☐☐ ☐☐ ☐■☐☐☐

2 ■☐☐☐☐☐☐☐

3 ☐☐☐ ☐☐■☐☐☐☐

4 ☐☐☐☐☐☐■ ☐☐☐☐☐☐☐

5 ☐☐■☐☐☐☐☐

6 ☐☐☐☐■

1 2 3 4 5 6

The mystery word is ______________ and it means ______________.

2 Decide which of these sentences refer to the present and which to the future. Write P or F.

a Les voitures seront interdites.

b Tu es pessimiste.

c Il y a beaucoup d'éoliennes.

d Il y aura des panneaux solaires.

e On recyclera l'eau.

f Ils recyclent les bouteilles.

g On cultivera des fruits.

h On habitera en ville.

i Les transports publics sont efficaces.

j La ville sera verte.

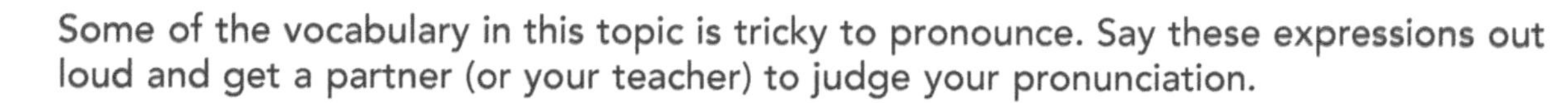

3 Some of the vocabulary in this topic is tricky to pronounce. Say these expressions out loud and get a partner (or your teacher) to judge your pronunciation.

l'immeuble	l'eau de pluie	le panneau solaire	il y aura
le toit	l'éolienne	pollué	efficace

4 Draw lines to link the French and English expressions.

a à mon avis	it's a good idea
b je pense que	I think that
c je crois que	I don't agree
d je suis d'accord	I hope that
e je ne suis pas d'accord	I believe that
f j'imagine que	in my opinion
g c'est une bonne idée	I agree
h j'espère que	I imagine that

5 In pairs. A makes a statement about the city of the future. B must disagree with A's statement, using an 'opinion' expression. Then swap roles.

Exemple

A Il y aura beaucoup de pollution.

B Je crois qu'il n'y aura pas de pollution.

6 Rewrite these sentences in the future tense.

a Il y a beaucoup de panneaux solaires. ______________________

b On cultive des légumes. ______________________

c La ville est polluée. ______________________

d Ils recyclent l'eau de pluie. ______________________

e C'est affreux! ______________________

f On respecte l'environnement. ______________________

7 Underline all the future tense verbs in the article.

Comment sera la ville de demain?

La ville de demain sera probablement polluée. Il y aura beaucoup de voitures et les rues seront dangereuses pour les cyclistes et les piétons. Il y aura trop de bruit, les immeubles seront laids et il y aura des graffitis partout. Mais cette opinion est peut-être trop pessimiste. Les optimistes pensent que la ville de demain sera très verte, avec des murs végétaux et beaucoup d'arbres. On espère qu'on cultivera des légumes sur les toits. On recyclera l'eau de pluie et on aura des éoliennes pour produire de l'électricité. Les transports publics seront très efficaces et il n'y aura pas de voitures dans les rues.

8 Copy out two pessimistic sentences and two optimistic sentences from the text.

Pessimistic: ______________________ Optimistic: ______________________

______________________ ______________________

9 Read the text in exercise 7 again. Write T (true) or F (false). ★

a Optimists think there will be lots of noise. ☐

b People will grow trees on their roofs. ☐

c People will produce electricity from recycled water. ☐

d Public transport will be efficient. ☐

e People will grow vegetables. ☐

f Pessimists think there won't be any cars. ☐

10 Translate the sentences you wrote in exercise 8 into English. ★

____

____

____

____

3 Topic 3 En danger

• Pupil Book pages 60–61

Aujourd' hui est  ________________________. Il est ________________.

Langue et grammaire

Negatives

In this topic, you'll come across three ways of making a sentence negative. This is called *negation*.

ne ... pas	not
ne ... rien	nothing
ne ... plus	not any more / no more

The first part of the negative construction comes before the verb, and the second part comes after the verb.

*La situation **n'**est **pas** catastrophique.*	The situation is not disastrous.
*Il **n'**y aura **plus** d'abeilles.*	There won't be any more bees.
*On **ne** fait **rien**.*	We do nothing.

Also remember not to use *un/une/du/de l'/des*, but *de* (or *d'* in front of a vowel) after negatives.

*Il n'y aura pas **de** problème.*	There won't be a problem.
*On ne trouvera plus **d'**ours.*	We won't find bears any more.

1 Write the French names of the animals next to the pictures. To help you, they are presented as anagrams in the box below.

liebael croohrsnié grite gnroa-unoat sour noth

a 

b

c 

d 

e 

f 

________ ________ ________ ________ ________ ________

2 What do the negative expressions in these sentences mean? Write 'not', 'nothing' or 'no more'.

a Il n'y aura plus d'abeilles. ________

b On ne fait pas attention. ________

c Je ne ferai rien. ________

d Il n'y a pas de problème. ________

e On ne trouvera plus d'ours bruns. ________

f Il n'y aura rien à faire. ________

g Je n'ai plus d'argent. ________

h On n'a rien trouvé. ________

3 In pairs. A asks for some items. B completes the phrase *Malheureusement, je n'ai plus de/d'...* to say that they haven't got any of the items any more. Then swap roles.

Exemple

A Tu as du pain?

B Malheureusement, je n'ai plus de pain.

4 Unjumble these sentences. They all use negative expressions about the future of species.

a n'y de Bientôt plus il baleines aura

____

b abeilles Si les ne disparaîtront on fait rien,

____

c sera sauver ours Bientôt les pour il tard trop

____

d ne il thon de plus rouge aura fait n'y Si attention, on pas

____

e plus ne On Inde tigres trouvera de en

____

f pandas de il aura quelques plus Dans n'y années,

____

5 Translate the unjumbled sentences from exercise 4 into English.

____

____

____

____

____

____

6 Translate these expressions into French.

a If we aren't careful... _______________

b Soon... _______________

c If we don't do anything... _______________

d In a few years' time... _______________

Identify these endangered species. Write a letter (a–h) next to each French phrase (1–8).

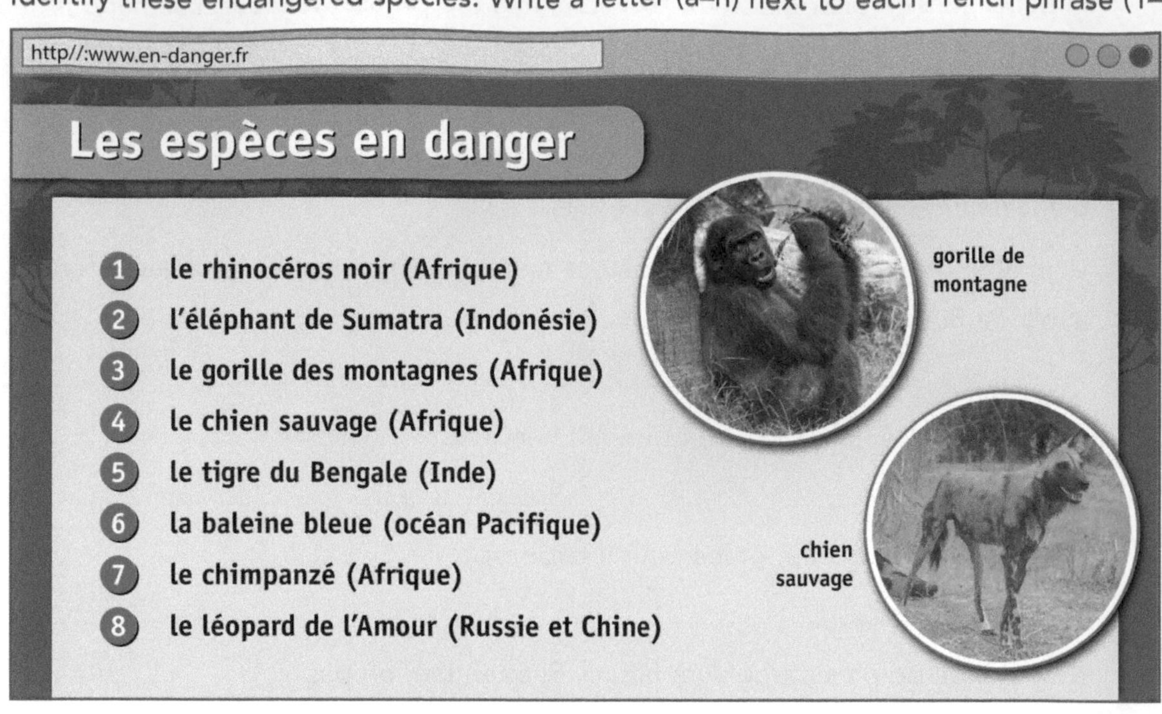

a chimpanzee ________ b black rhino ________ c mountain gorilla ________

d wild dog ________ e blue whale ________ f Bengal tiger ________

g Amur leopard ________ h Sumatran elephant ________

8 Write a suitable sentence about each of the endangered animals listed in exercise 7. Start each sentence with an expression translated from exercise 6.

You can use the introductory expressions in any order you like. Be careful, because the sentences can get quite complicated. Use the future tense accurately and include negative expressions such as *ne … pas*, *ne … rien* and *ne … plus*.

____

____

____

____

____

____

____

____

Topic 4 L'art de la récupération

- Pupil Book pages 62–63

Aujourd' hui est  ______________________. Il est  ______________.

Langue et grammaire

The present participle

In English, to express the fact that two actions are happening at the same time or are related, we say 'while' or 'by' and use the *–ing* form of the verb. In French, you use *en* together with a form of the verb called the present participle.

*Elle a eu cette idée **en regardant** un documentaire.*	She had that idea while watching a documentary.

To make the present participle, you normally take the *nous* form of the verb in the present tense, remove the *–ons* ending, and replace it with *–ant.*

*travailler → nous travaillons → **en travaillant***

*Elle chante **en travaillant***	She sings while working.

*utiliser → nous utilisons → **utilisant***

*Il sauve de l'eau **en utilisant** l'eau de pluie dans le jardin.*	He saves water by using rainwater in the garden.

Pronunciation

Notice how the different verb endings are pronounced. The ending *–ant* rhymes with *cent* and the ending *–ons* rhymes with *non.*

Write the present participle (*–ant*) of these verbs.

a regarder	______________	b travailler	______________
c fabriquer	______________	d jouer	______________
e utiliser	______________	f recycler	______________
g donner	______________	h lire	______________
i acheter	______________	j prendre	______________

Unjumble the words and write them next to the appropriate pictures.

erevr ref uae sobi utilspaqe reappi otracn

1  ______________

2  ______________

3 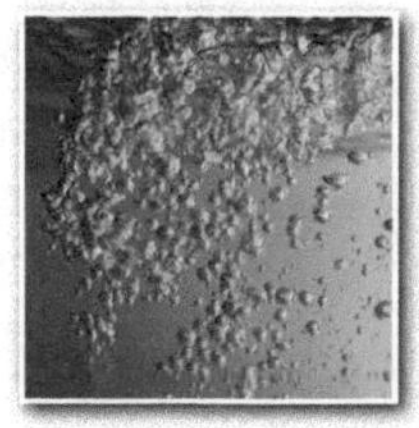 ______________

4  ______________

5  ______________

6 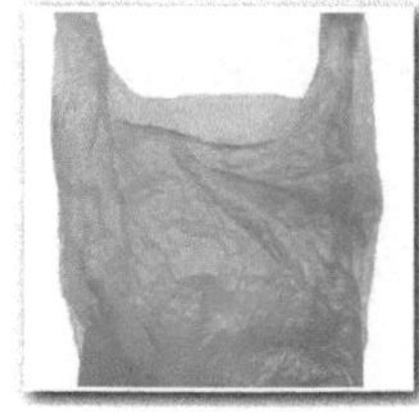 ______________

7  ______________

3 Join the two sentences together, using a present participle construction (*en …ant*).

a Abdou chante. Il travaille.

Abdou chante en travaillant.

b Sophie fait ses devoirs. Elle regarde la télévision.

____

c Pierre a fait une sculpture. Il a utilisé du fer.

____

d On ne conduit pas. On regarde son portable.

____

e Je protège l'environnement. Je recycle mes bouteilles.

____

f Je fais du jogging. J'écoute de la musique.

____

g Marc a passé le temps. Il a lu un livre.

____

h J'ai trouvé des déchets recyclables. J'ai rangé ma maison.

____

4 Any text that you read may contain vocabulary you don't know, but it is always possible to work out or guess its meaning or to look it up. Read the article and find words with these meanings.

La maison recyclée

Cette petite maison a coûté moins de 200 euros! Le fermier Michael Buck a construit la maison en utilisant des méthodes anciennes de construction. En prenant du sable, de la paille, de l'eau et de la boue, il a construit une maison recyclée. Il a créé les fenêtres en récupérant le pare-brise d'un vieux camion! Il a trouvé le bois pour le plancher en triant la benne d'un voisin. La maison est même chaude en hiver: M. Buck a isolé les murs en utilisant la laine de ses moutons!

a sand ________ b straw ________ c mud ________

d windscreen ________ e lorry ________ f floor ________

g skip ________ h neighbour ________ i wood ________

j sheep ________

5 Re-read the text in exercise 4 and underline all the present participle constructions.

6 In pairs. A reads out all the expressions underlined in exercise 5. B assesses how well they are pronounced. Then swap roles.

7 Translate the first three sentences of exercise 4 (up to *recyclée*) into English.

8 Go back to exercise 3. Translate all the sentences you have created into English.

9 Translate these sentences into French.

a I understand French by using a dictionary.

b We go into town by taking the bus.

c The artist made a sculpture by recycling glass and wood.

Construisez un mobile génial en recyclant des fourchettes, des cuillères et des couteaux en métal!

3 Topic 5 S'engager

• Pupil Book pages 64–65

Aujourd' hui est  ______________________. Il est  ______________.

Langue et grammaire

Impersonal expressions

Here are some expressions you will come across in this topic. They are called impersonal expressions because they don't refer to a specific person or thing.

Il faut means 'it is necessary' and is directly followed by a verb in the infinitive.

Il faut sauver l'environnement. — It is necessary to save the environment.

C'est can be used with an adjective followed by *de* and a verb in the infinitive:

C'est possible de combattre la pauvreté. — It is possible to beat poverty.

C'est difficile d'ignorer le problème. — It is difficult to ignore the problem.

C'est facile d'aider en organisant une collecte. — It is easy to help with a collection.

1 Not all these words mean what they seem to. Circle the correct meaning.

a à mon avis = following my advice / in my opinion

b maladie = illness / melody

c spectacle = pair of glasses / show

d temps = time / part-time workers

e ado = teenager / fuss

f faire passer = to let someone pass / to get across

g exposition = exposure / exhibition

h s'engager = to get involved / to get engaged

i faim = fame / hunger

j donner = to give / kebab

2 Insert the equivalents of the words in brackets.

a Il ________ lutter contre la pauvreté. (*is necessary*)

b C'est ________ d'aider les enfants. (*important*)

c C'est ________ de sauver l'environnement. (*possible*)

d C'est ________ de faire une collecte. (*easy*)

e C'est ________ de défendre les droits humains. (*difficult*)

f Il ________ combattre les maladies. (*is necessary*)

3 Match the speech bubbles to the charitable organisations. Write a number 1–6.

1 Les Amis de la Terre ◄ Les Amis de la Terre

2 AMNESTY INTERNATIONAL — Amnesty International ▲

3 unicef — ▲ L'UNICEF

4 MEDECINS SANS FRONTIERES DOCTORS WITHOUT BORDERS — ▲ Médecins Sans Frontières

5 ACTION CONTRE LA FAIM — ◄ Action contre la Faim

6 CONTRE LE CANCER LA LIGUE pour la vie — ◄ La Ligue contre le cancer

a Mon grand-père est mort du cancer du poumon, et c'est pour ça que je m'engage pour cette cause. ______

b Je m'engage pour cette organisation parce qu'il est important de protéger les enfants. ______

c À mon avis, il est important de secourir les victimes de catastrophes naturelles. ______

d Il faut protéger l'environnement. ______

e Il est difficile (mais possible) de défendre les droits humains. ______

f Je soutiens cette cause parce que des millions de personnes dans le monde n'ont pas assez à manger. ______

4 In pairs. A chooses a phrase from column 1 and reads it out. B adds a verb from column 2. A completes the sentence with an appropriate phrase from column 3. Then swap roles.

Il est important/possible/difficile/facile/nécessaire de… Il faut …	lutter protéger sauver combattre	les enfants le cancer pour les droits humains l'environnement

5 Go back to exercise 3. Translate all the sentences in the speech bubbles into English. ★

____

____

____

____

____

____

6 Read this charity leaflet. Are the statements about it true (T), false (F) or not mentioned (NM)?

SOUTENEZ LES ORGANISATIONS CARITATIVES

Il est important de penser de temps en temps aux personnes qui mènent une vie difficile. Il y a des pays où les enfants doivent travailler quatorze heures par jour et où leurs parents n'ont que du riz à manger. Il y a un risque constant d'attraper des maladies mortelles, du fait de l'absence d'eau potable dans un environnement pollué. Dans certains pays, on peut être emprisonné parce qu'on n'est pas d'accord avec le gouvernement. Et des ouragans, des famines et des tsunamis peuvent détruire des villes entières. Il est facile d'ignorer ces catastrophes, mais il est possible aussi de soutenir une ou plusieurs organisations caritatives.

PENSEZ-Y!

a You should constantly think about people with hard lives. ☐

b Some children have to work long hours. ☐

c Their parents have plenty to eat. ☐

d Lack of clean drinking water can lead to fatal illnesses. ☐

e Pollution is caused by CO_2 emissions. ☐

f Some government ministers are sent to prison. ☐

g Entire towns can be wiped out by natural disasters. ☐

h It's easy not to think about these things. ☐

i You should only support one charity. ☐

j You should think about it. ☐

7 Find the French for these words in the text in exercise 5.

a life ______________

b drinkable ______________

c polluted ______________

d imprisoned ______________

e hurricanes ______________

f to support ______________

8 Choose a charitable organisation. It can be one mentioned in this topic or one of your choice. Write a few lines to encourage people to support it. Use expressions such as *Il est important/facile/possible de…* and *Il faut…* ★

____

____

____

3 Topic 6 Pour ou contre les robots?

• Pupil Book pages 66–67

Aujourd' hui est  ______________________. Il est  ______________.

Langue et grammaire

Indefinite pronouns

When you need phrases such as 'everyone', 'someone', 'no one' or 'something', use one of the following pronouns:

tout le monde	everyone	*quelque chose*	something
quelqu'un	someone	*personne*	nobody

Quelqu'un and *quelque chose* can followed by either *de* + adjective or *qui* + verb:

quelqu'un de gentil	someone kind.
quelque chose de ridicule	something ridiculous
quelque chose qui coûte cher	something that costs a lot

Do not confuse *personne* and *une personne*:

personne	nobody
une personne	a person

When *personne* is used as a pronoun it is used with *ne*, always placed directly before the verb.

*Personne **ne** veut do faire les courses.*	Nobody wants to the shopping.
*Je **ne** vois personne.*	I don't see anybody.

Match the French and English sentences.

1 Personne n'aime les robots.
2 Qui est arrivé? Personne.
3 Trois personnes sont arrivées.
4 Je n'ai rencontré personne.

a Three people have arrived.
b Who's arrived? No one.
c No one likes robots.
d I didn't meet anyone.

Adapt the sentences from exercise 1 to make French sentences with these meanings.

a We didn't see anyone.

____

b Who hates chocolate? No one.

____

c There are two people in the kitchen.

____

d No one likes my brother.

____

Write in *de* or *qui*.

a quelqu'un ________ fabrique des robots
b quelque chose ________ est très facile
c quelque chose ________ difficile
d quelqu'un ________ généreux
e quelque chose ________ drôle
f quelqu'un ________ mange beaucoup

Read the text and find the French for these words.

a washing up ________ b lawnmower ________ c lawn ________

d vacuum cleaner ________ e factory ________ f soon ________

Les robots existent déjà! On peut acheter une tondeuse à gazon qui coupe la pelouse pendant qu'on se détend. C'est très fort, comme machine. Ce robot peut éviter les plantes, les arbres, même les chats! Il y a aussi un robot en forme d'aspirateur. Si quelqu'un n'a pas envie de passer l'aspirateur, ce robot fonctionne tout seul. Et bien sûr, les usines sont pleines de robots qui fabriquent des voitures et des ordinateurs. Est-ce qu'il existe des robots pour faire la vaisselle ou pour ranger la chambre? Pas encore, mais c'est quelque chose de possible – peut-être bientôt!

Re-read the text in exercise 4 and answer 'yes' or 'no'.

a Are there robots that make your bed? ________

b Are there robots that make cars? ________

c Are there robots that do the washing up? ________

d Are there robots that mow the lawn? ________

e Are there robots that do the vacuuming? ________

f Are there robots that make computers? ________

6 In pairs. A says an impersonal pronoun. B has to come up with a sentence using it. Repeat for each of the pronouns listed and then swap roles.

quelqu'un quelque chose tout le monde personne

Exemple

A tout le monde

B Tout le monde aime les robots.

7 Read the article and answer the questions. ★

Shopi

Des scientifiques chinois ont inventé un robot capable de faire les courses. Il s'appelle **Shopi**. Tout le monde peut travailler facilement avec Shopi.
Si quelqu'un lui donne une liste de courses sur une clé USB, Shopi va au supermarché, trouve les articles, paye avec une carte de crédit et rentre à la maison avec les choses qu'il a achetées.
Et si on oublie quelque chose? Pas de problème. On peut téléphoner à Shopi. Il a un portable et il comprend l'anglais, le français et le mandarin.

a What does Shopi do? ____________________

b Who invented him? ____________________

c How do you program him? ____________________

d How does he pay? ____________________

e What if you forget something? ____________________

f Do you think the article tells a true story? ____________________

8 Invent a useful robot. Write a few lines in French explaining what your robot can do. ★

____

____

____

____

4 Topic 1 La liberté de choisir

• Pupil Book pages 80–81

Aujourd' hui est  ______________________________ . Il est  ______________________ .

Langue et grammaire

Prepositions

A preposition can be used with a verb to complete its meaning. Make sure you learn the preposition with the verb. It's important to remember that any verb which immediately follows a preposition must be used in the infinitive form.

J'ai commencé à apprendre le français à l'âge de 10 ans.	I started to learn French at the age of 10.
J'essaie de manger moins de bonbons.	I'm trying to eat fewer sweets.

Some verbs do not need to be followed by a preposition.

J'adore chanter.	I love to sing.

Pronunciation

Notice how *ch* in French is the same as 'sh' in English. Practise saying these three words:

chambre *choisir* *chaussures*

Decide whether these verbs are followed by *de* or *à*. Circle the correct preposition. Then draw a line to the correct English meaning.

a avoir peur **de** / **à**	to try to
b apprendre **de** / **à**	to continue to
c choisir **de** / **à**	to have the right to
d avoir envie **de** / **à**	to be afraid to
e commencer **de** / **à**	to start to
f essayer **de** / **à**	to learn to
g avoir le droit **de** / **à**	to decide to
h arrêter **de** / **à**	to want to
i décider **de** / **à**	to choose to
j continuer **de** / **à**	to stop doing

In pairs. A reads out these words which contain *oi*. B assesses how well pronounced the words are.

fois Poirot loi quoi choix toi boire doit vouloir moi

Now B reads out these words which contain *ch* and A assesses.

chambre choisir chat cher chaussette chic chômage chanson chez

Read what these people say and fill in the grid.

Jamila: J'ai le droit de sortir le week-end, mais je n'ai pas le droit de regarder les sites de réseaux sociaux pendant les repas.

Simon: Mes parents sont stricts. Je n'ai pas le droit de choisir à quelle heure je me couche, mais j'ai le droit de faire mes devoirs – hélas!

Camille: Moi, j'ai de la chance, car mes parents sont plutôt relax. J'ai le droit de me maquiller et de choisir tous mes vêtements. Mais je n'ai pas le droit de choisir où aller pendant les vacances. Ça, c'est le choix de mes parents.

Jamila Simon Camille

	Allowed to	Not allowed to
Jamila		
Simon		
Camille		

4 Write down, in French, three things you are allowed to do and three things you aren't allowed to do. They don't have to be true but you must use the expression *avoir le droit de…* and the infinitive.

____

____

____

____

____

____

Read this article about a boy who used to be lacking in confidence. Underline all the verb + preposition + infinitive expressions.

Avoir confiance

Un garçon qui s'appelait Didier avait peur de sortir tout seul, parce qu'il était très inquiet. Un jour, il a eu envie d'aller à la piscine avec des copains mais les autres ont décidé de rester à la maison. Ils ont choisi de regarder un film à la télé. Didier a essayé de quitter la maison mais il n'a pas réussi. "J'ai le droit de sortir seul", pensait-il, et sa mère était d'accord avec lui. "Si tu as envie de sortir, pourquoi pas?" Alors Didier a pris le bus et il a appris à sortir seul. Ce n'était pas tellement difficile. Il a continué à être courageux et maintenant il n'a plus peur.

6 Re-read the article in exercise 5 and answer these questions.

a What was Didier's problem?

____

b What did he want to do?

____

c What went wrong?

____

d Why?

____

e What did he think about it?

____

f What did his mother think?

____

g So what did Didier do?

____

h What's the situation now?

____

7 Write in the correct past participle and preposition. The past participles are provided below to help you.

continué décidé choisi commencé arrêté essayé eu appris

a Sophie a ________ ________ faire de la danse. (*decided to*)

b Elle a ________ ________ faire aussi de la natation. (*chose to*)

c Manon a ________ ________ manger des légumes. (*started to*)

d Elle a aussi ________ ________ faire du sport. (*learned to*)

e Abdou a ________ ________ sortir seul. (*tried to*)

f Ses parents ont ________ ________ dire 'non'. (*continued to*)

g Justine a ________ envie ________ jouer au tennis. (*wanted to*)

h Sophie a ________ ________ faire de la danse. (*stopped*)

8 Translate into French: ★

a I want to go out at the weekend. ______________________

b Thomas decided to play on the computer. ______________________

c We learned to ride a bike. ______________________

d The teacher started to speak. ______________________

e The girls stopped eating meat. ______________________

9 Write: ★

- one thing you have started to do

____

- one thing you have stopped doing

____

- one thing you want to do

____

Quelle voie choisir?

• Pupil Book pages 82–83

Aujourd' hui est ______________________. Il est ______________.

Langue et grammaire

The future tense

- Use the future tense to talk about what you will do or what will happen. To form the future tense of regular verbs, take the infinitive and add these endings (remove the 'e' from *–re* verbs first):
  je *–ai* *tu* *–as* *il/elle/on* *–a*
- Some verbs have an irregular stem in the future tense. Here is a reminder of some important ones:

faire	to do	*fer–*	*Je ferai du français / de la musique / des maths.*	I will do French / music / maths.
être	to be	*ser–*	*Tu seras en 3ᵉ.*	You will be in year 10.
avoir	to have	*aur–*	*Il aura le droit de choisir.*	He will have the right to choose.
aller	to go	*ir–*	*Elle ira au lycée professionnel.*	She will go to the *lycée professionnel*.

- Sometimes the future tense is used in French when the present tense is used in English. For example:
  Quand je serai plus grand j'aurai le droit de choisir. When I am bigger I will have the right to choose.

1 Insert the correct future verb forms.

a Je ________ mes études à l'université. (*faire*)

b Elle ________ au lycée professionnel. (*aller*)

c L'année prochaine, Rachid ________ en troisième. (*être*)

d Lola ________ à faire de l'anglais. (*continuer*)

e Mais elle ________ de faire de la musique. (*arrêter*)

f Manon ________ au lycée général. (*aller*)

g Je ________ bien dans mes baskets. (*être*)

h Tu ________ le droit de choisir tes matières. (*avoir*)

i J' ________ de la chance. (*avoir*)

j Thomas ________ le collège. (*quitter*)

2 Use English words to explain these French expressions to do with education. You may need to use several words.

a obligatoire ______________

b troisième ______________

c le baccalauréat ______________

d les études supérieures ______________

e quatrième ______________

f le système scolaire ______________

Read Olly's plans for next year. Put ticks in the appropriate columns.

e-mail

Sujet: matières

Pour: antoine-1@frmail.fr

Salut Antoine,
Ici en Angleterre, on a le droit de choisir certaines matières quand on est en year 10 (la troisième). Moi, l'année prochaine, je continuerai à faire des maths – malheureusement, parce que je n'aime pas ça – et aussi de l'anglais et des sciences. Ces matières sont obligatoires. Il y a trois autres matières que je n'aime pas: la musique, l'espagnol et l'informatique. J'arrêterai de faire de la musique et de l'espagnol mais je continuerai à faire de l'informatique parce que c'est très utile aujourd'hui. J'adore la technologie, donc je continuerai à en faire, mais j'arrêterai de faire des arts plastiques parce que je ne suis pas très fort. Je continuerai à faire de l'EPS parce que c'est obligatoire.
Amitiés,
Olly

Subject	Giving up	Carrying on
Maths		
English		
Science		
Music		
Spanish		
ICT		
Technology		
Art		
Sport		

Re-read the text in exercise 3 and choose the correct options.

a Olly est **français** / **anglais**.

b Il est en **quatrième** / **troisième**.

c L'année prochaine il sera en **quatrième** / **troisième**.

d Il **aime** / **n'aime pas** les maths.

e L'anglais **est** / **n'est pas** obligatoire.

f Il **aime bien** / **n'aime pas** l'espagnol.

g Il **continuera** à faire / **arrêtera de faire de** l'informatique.

h Il arrêtera de faire **des arts plastiques** / **de la technologie**.

i Il continuera à faire **des arts plastiques** / **de la technologie.**

j Il **a** / **n'a pas** le droit d'arrêter de faire de l'EPS.

Note down six subjects and whether you plan to give them up or not. Ask and answer questions with your partner.

Exemple

A Tu continueras à faire du français?

B Non, j'arrêterai de faire du français.

Translate these phrases, using the future tense for the English present. Complete the sentences as well, if you can.

a When I am bigger… ______________________

b When I leave secondary school… ______________________

c When I choose my subjects… ______________________

d When I stop doing maths… ______________________

e When I do my homework… ______________________

7 Translate this article into English. ★

For the purposes of this topic, call a *collège* a secondary school and a *lycée* a high school.

le collège

En France, quand on finit le collège, ce n'est pas comme en Angleterre. On n'a pas le droit de choisir ses matières. On doit choisir un lycée pour passer le bac. Si on veut travailler après le lycée, il faut choisir un lycée professionnel, mais si on veut continuer ses études à l'université, il faut choisir un lycée général. Le choix est difficile pour les jeunes, mais on n'a pas le droit d'arrêter de passer plusieurs matières (comme en Angleterre).

____

____

____

____

____

____

8 Using a separate piece of paper, write about which subjects you will carry on with and which ones you will drop next year. Use: *Je continuerai à faire…*, *J'arrêterai de faire…* and *Je ferai…* Also give reasons, using *parce que…* ★

4 Topic 3 Mon argent de poche

- Pupil Book pages 84–85

Aujourd' hui est  ______________________________ . Il est  ____________________ .

Langue et grammaire

Frequency

- To talk about how often something happens or is done, use *par* to mean 'per':

par semaine	per week
par mois	per month
par an	per year

- To say 'every two days', 'every three weeks' and so on, use *tous les* for masculine nouns and *toutes les* for feminine nouns:

tous les deux jours	every two days
toutes les trois semaines	every three weeks

Future tense

You'll see a few more verbs being used in the future tense in this topic. Notice that *recevoir* (to receive, to get) and *acheter* (to buy) both have irregular future stems:

Le mois prochain je recevrai 15€.	Next month, I will get €15.
J'achèterai un tee-shirt.	I'll buy a T-shirt.

Translate these time expressions into English.

a 350€ par semaine ____________________

b deux fois par mois ____________________

c quatre fois par an ____________________

d tous les mois ____________________

e toutes les semaines ____________________

f tous les trois jours ____________________

g 50€ par jour ____________________

h 8€ par heure ____________________

How much pocket money do these people get? Write out the amounts in figures.

Je reçois vingt-cinq euros par semaine.

____

Je reçois cent euros par mois.

____

Je reçois quinze euros toutes les deux semaines.

____

Je reçois deux cents euros tous les six mois.

____

Je reçois dix euros par jour.

____

Je reçois cinq cents euros par an.

____

3 Say how you earn your pocket money, following the example.

a 

Pour gagner mon argent de poche, je passe l'aspirateur.

b 

____

c 

____

d 

____

e 

____

f 

____

4 Play a guessing game in pairs. A chooses an amount of money and a frequency among those given below. B guesses how much pocket money A receives, and how often. Then swap roles.

Exemple

A Tu reçois 50 euros par mois?

B Non. / Oui, je reçois 50 euros par mois!

20 euros | 75 euros | 50 euros | 5 euros | 100 euros

par semaine | par mois | toutes les deux semaines | par jour | tous les deux mois

5 Read this text and circle V (*vrai*) or F (*faux*).

a Fatima ne reçoit pas d'argent de poche. V / F

b Elle dépense tout son argent. V / F

c Elle dépense quelques euros. V / F

d Elle passera les vacances à la maison. V / F

e Elle travaille pour gagner son argent. V / F

f Elle a un compte bancaire. V / F

Quand maman me donne mon argent de poche, je vais en ville et j'achète des trucs. Je dépense quelques euros pour acheter des vêtements ou des chaussures. Mais je ne dépense pas tout mon argent. J'économise pour les vacances d'été, que je passe en Italie. Je verse alors cinquante euros par mois sur mon compte bancaire.

6 Rewrite the text in exercise 5 using the future tense. Start: *Quand Maman me donnera…* ★

____

____

____

____

7 Now translate the text you have just written (in the future tense) into English. ★

____

____

____

____

8 Answer these questions for yourself, using full sentences where possible. Add in extra information if you want. ★

a Tu gagnes combien d'argent de poche?

____

b Qu'est-ce que tu fais pour gagner ton argent?

____

c Tu dépenses combien d'argent?

____

d Qu'est-ce que tu achètes?

____

e As-tu un compte bancaire?

____

f Est-ce que tu économises?

____

g Pourquoi ou pourquoi pas?

____

h Tu es plutôt dépensier/ère ou économe?

____

4 Topic 4 Faire du bénévolat

• Pupil Book pages 86–87

Aujourd' hui est  ______________________ . Il est  ______________ .

Langue et grammaire

Suggesting what people could do

To suggest what people could do, you can use the verb *pouvoir* (to be able) in the conditional tense.

je pourrais	I could
tu pourrais	you could
il/elle pourrait	he/she could

Remember to use the infinitive of the verb that follows *pouvoir*. Look at these examples:

Je pourrais aider des enfants.	I could help children.
Tu pourrais nettoyer la voiture.	You could wash the car.
Il pourrait donner des cours de français.	He could give French lessons.

 Draw lines to link these French infinitives with their English meanings.

a s'inscrire à	to meet
b enrichir	to mow
c tondre	to share
d rencontrer	to join
e utiliser	to use
f transmettre	to enhance
g partager	to visit
h rendre visite à	to pass on
i donner des cours	to get involved
j s'engager	to give lessons

 Fill in the grid with words from this topic.

1 □□□■□□□□□□□

2 □□□□□□□■□

3 □□□■□□□□□□□

4 □□□□■

5 □□□□□■□□

6 □□□□□■□□

7 □■□□□□□□

1 skills
2 volunteer work
3 voluntary organisation
4 lesson
5 post
6 volunteer
7 to enhance

The mystery word is ______________ .

3 Write in *pourrais* or *pourrait*.

a Je __________ donner des cours de sport.

b Il __________ donner des cours de musique.

c Elle __________ rendre visite à une personne âgée.

d Tu __________ tondre la pelouse.

e Sophie __________ donner des cours de français.

f Manon __________ donner des cours d'anglais.

4 Which of the people in exercise 3 would be able to help these people? Write a letter a–f.

1 une fille qui voudrait jouer du violon

2 une famille africaine qui vient d'arriver en France

3 un garçon qui veut apprendre à jouer au tennis

4 une famille qui voudrait passer ses vacances à Londres

5 une personne qui est trop vieille pour faire du jardinage

6 une personne qui habite seule

5 Who are these people? Write in a number.

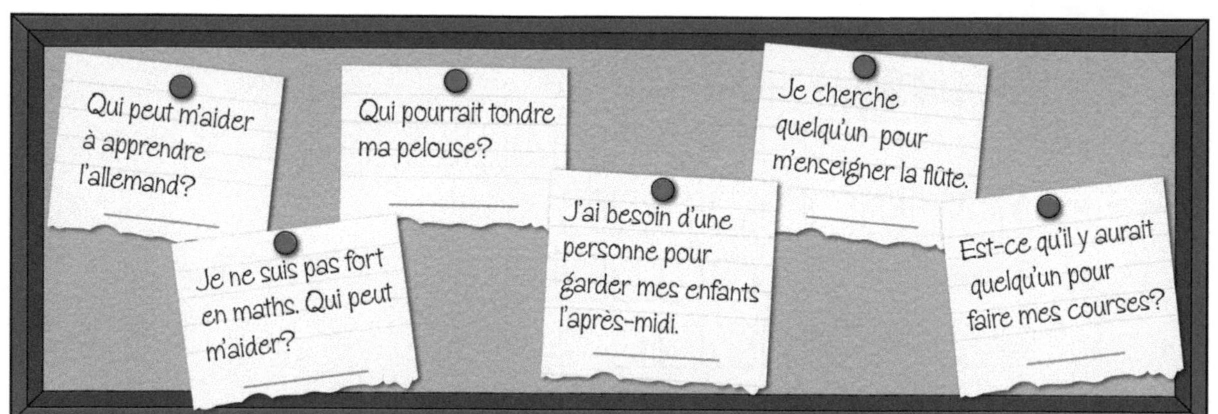

1 someone who needs maths coaching

2 someone too old to mow the lawn

3 an old lady who can't manage to do her own shopping

4 someone who wants music lessons

5 someone with childcare problems

6 someone who wants to visit Berlin

In pairs, think aloud. What sort of voluntary work could you do? Take turns to speak, starting with *Je pourrais...* Don't restrict yourself to vocabulary from this topic: think about your personal talents and use your imagination to come up with unusual activities. If you need help with vocabulary, use a dictionary or ask your teacher.

Translate this leaflet into English. ★

Qu'est-ce qu'on pourrait faire pour être utile aux autres dans notre société? Tout le monde a des compétences qu'il ou elle pourrait partager avec d'autres qui ont des difficultés dans la vie. Par exemple, près de chez toi, il y a certainement des personnes âgées que tu pourrais aider dans le jardin ou avec le ménage. Ou bien il y a probablement des enfants que tu pourrais aider en donnant des cours de musique, de dessin, de sport. Regarde dans le journal de ta région pour identifier des associations qui cherchent des bénévoles.

8 Set out some ideas for the sort of voluntary work you could do. Try to use complex sentences like the one in the example. ★

Mon talent est la musique, donc je pourrais aider des enfants à apprendre à chanter.

4 Topic 5 Plus tard je serai...

- Pupil Book pages 88–89

Aujourd' hui est  ______________________. Il est  ______________.

Langue et grammaire

Talking about jobs

The indefinite article (*un* or *une*) is not used when you are talking about what job someone does:

Je suis journaliste.	I am a journalist.
Il est acteur.	He is an actor.

Talking about what you will do in the future

You already know when and how to use the future tense but here's a reminder. Use the future tense to talk about what you will do or what will happen in the future. You form the future tense of regular *–er* and *–ir* verbs by adding these endings to the infinitive:

je	*–ai*
tu	*–as*
il/elle	*–a*

For example:

Plus tard je mangerai une glace.	Later I will eat an ice cream.
Demain il parlera avec le professeur.	Tomorrow he will speak with the teacher.

For regular *–re* verbs, you use the same endings but you make the stem by only removing the 'e' from the end of the infinitive. For example:

L'année prochaine j'apprendrai l'espagnol.	Next year, I will learn Spanish.

Remember that you will see a few irregular stems. For example, *je serai* means 'I will be'.

Find eight French words for jobs in this wordsearch. To help you, the English words are given beside the wordsearch.

i	n	f	i	r	m	i	è	r	e
m	d	g	k	m	a	b	l	j	c
j	o	u	r	é	g	g	ê	n	f
c	o	i	f	d	e	h	a	f	e
p	r	o	f	e	s	s	e	u	r
i	è	r	e	c	i	s	t	e	m
e	p	o	l	i	c	i	e	r	i
i	n	g	e	n	i	e	u	r	e
p	l	o	m	b	i	e	r	i	r
t	e	c	h	n	i	c	i	e	n

farmer
nurse
teacher
policeman
doctor
engineer
technician
plumber

Use the vocabulary in the wordsearch to play a guessing game with a partner. First write down the job you have chosen (but don't show it to your partner) so that you can prove you aren't cheating. Then swap roles.

Exemple

A Plus tard, tu seras infirmière?

B Non, plus tard, je serai technicienne.

3 Add a logical job to each sentence.

Remember, the form of the word may be different depending on whether you are male or female.

Je réparerai des machines dans une usine. *Je serai ingénieur.*

a J'enseignerai l'anglais à des enfants. ______

b Je travaillerai dans un hôpital. ______

c Je réparerai des machines à laver. ______

d J'arrêterai des criminels. ______

e Je cultiverai des fruits et des légumes. ______

4 Translate the sentences in exercise 3 into English, including the words you have added.

______

______

______

______

______

______

______

______

______

Are these ambitions realistic or unrealistic? Write R or U.

a Je gagnerai une médaille d'or aux Jeux olympiques. [ ]

b Je serai champion du monde d'échecs. [ ]

c Je serai professeur d'anglais. [ ]

d Je travaillerai dans la cuisine d'un restaurant. [ ]

e Je serai astronaute. [ ]

f Je travaillerai dans un magasin. [ ]

6 Read these sentences and fill in the most appropriate job from the box below.

policière | prof d'EPS | magicien | actrice | agent de voyages

a Je suis sportive et travailleuse.
Je serai ______.

b Je suis amusant et agile.
Je serai ______.

c Je suis courageuse et juste.
Je serai ______.

d Je suis très extravertie.
Je serai ______.

e J'aime visiter les pays étrangers.
Je serai ______.

7 Translate the completed sentences in exercise 6 into English. ★

______

______

______

______

______

8 Now write a few lines about your real ambitions for the future. Give reasons and explanations and use some of the adjectives from exercise 6. ★

______

______

______

______

- Pupil Book pages 90–91

Aujourd' hui est  ______________________________ . Il est  ____________________ .

Langue et grammaire

Using the conditional

You've already seen that the conditional is used to talk about what you could do. You also use the conditional to talk about what you would do or what would happen.

You will see the conditional of regular *–er* and *–ir* verbs with these endings added to the infinitive:

je *–ais* *tu* *–ais* *il/elle* *–ait*

For example:

Si je pouvais, je voyagerais autour du monde. If I could, I would travel round the world.

For regular *–re* verbs, you will see the same endings but you make the stem by only removing the 'e' from the end of the infinitive. For example:

Je prendrais une décision plus facilement avec ton aide. I would make a decision more easily with your help.

Unjumble these words, which appear in this topic. Then draw a line to the English meaning.

retogû	______________	cure
aeimlad	______________	beauty
dèrmee	______________	to taste
éaubet	______________	future
nniotcmaé	______________	illness
rnaevi	______________	contaminated

Decide whether these verbs are in the present, future or conditional. Tick the appropriate column.

verb	present	future	conditional	verb	present	future	conditional
1 regarde				2 voyagerait			
3 prendrait				4 essayes			
5 essayerais				6 prendra			
7 regarderais				8 essayerai			
9 prend				10 voyagerai			
11 regarderais				12 voyages			

3 Write the *je/tu* and il/elle conditional forms of these verbs.

	verb	conditional (je/tu)	conditional (il/elle)
1	pouvoir	______	______
2	prendre	______	______
3	finir	______	______
4	regarder	______	______
5	jouer	______	______
6	aller	______	______
7	trouver	______	______
8	goûter	______	______
9	essayer	______	______
10	gagner	______	______

4 Insert the conditional verbs. The correct infinitives are given in brackets.

Je travaille tous les jours dans un bureau. C'est bien dommage. Si j'avais plus de temps, je ______ (*passer*) plus de temps avec ma femme et mes enfants. Je ______ (*voyager*) avec eux, peut-être en Afrique. Si je gagnais plus d'argent, j' ______ (*acheter*) des cadeaux pour ma famille et peut-être une nouvelle voiture. Je ______ (*faire*) plus de sports, cela ______ (*être*) bon pour ma santé. Et si je gagnais au loto, je ______ (*donner*) de l'argent à des associations qui aident les familles qui n'ont pas assez à manger. Mais ce n'est qu'un rêve!

5 Translate the exercise 4 text into English, starting with *Si j'avais plus de temps...*

____

____

____

____

____

____

6 Take a moment to prepare your answers to these questions.

- Qu'est-ce que tu ferais si tu avais le temps?
- Qu'est-ce que tu ferais si tu avais beaucoup d'argent?

Now take turns with a partner to ask and answer the questions. Try to develop conversations, using: *Vraiment? C'est tout? Tu as d'autres idées? Pourquoi?* etc.

7 Translate these conditional sentences into French. ★

a I would protect the environment. ______________________

b I would construct a tourist village. ______________________

c I would swim in the sea. ______________________

d Sarah would find a remedy for her allergy. ______________________

e Hugo would live in Vietnam. ______________________

f He would write a letter. ______________________

8 What would you do if you could? Write a few lines saying what you would do personally and what you would do to improve the world. Use vocabulary from this topic in the Pupil Book. If you need more verbs, use a dictionary or ask your teacher. ★

5 Topic 1 Quelle appli?

• Pupil Book pages 104–105

Aujourd' hui est ______________________. Il est ______________.

Langue et grammaire

Si…

The French for 'if' is si. You can use si to talk about what would happen if something else were the case. To do this, use the imperfect tense followed by the conditional tense.

*Si j'**avais** cette appli, je **serais** très content.* If I had this app, I would be very happy.

To make the conditional, use the same stem as for the future tense but with the verb endings of the imperfect.

infinitive	translation	future	imperfect	conditional
avoir	to have	*j'aurai*	*j'avais*	*j'aurais*
être	to be	*je serai*	*j'étais*	*je serais*
faire	to do/to make	*je ferai*	*je faisais*	*je ferais*
vouloir	to want	*je voudrai*	*je voulais*	*je voudrais*
jouer	to play	*je jouerai*	*je jouais*	*je jouerais*
choisir	to choose	*je choisirai*	*je choisissais*	*je choisirais*

Decide whether these verbs are in the future, imperfect or conditional tense. Put a tick in the appropriate column.

verb	future	imperfect	conditional	verb	future	imperfect	conditional
a je jouerai				b j'avais			
c je roulais				d j'aurais			
e je voudrais				f je serai			
g je serais				h je jouais			
i je jouerais				j je choisissais			
k je choisirais				l je ferai			
m je ferais				n j'aurais			
o j'étais							

2 Take all the verbs from exercise 1 and write them in the *il/elle* form.

a il/elle jouera ____________ b ____________

c ____________ d ____________

e ____________ f ____________

g ____________ h ____________

i ____________ j ____________

k ____________ l ____________

m ____________ n ____________

o ____________

3 Decide which of these apps is being described. Write a letter in the box beside each logo.

a Vous avez faim? Avec cette appli vous pouvez trouver tous les restaurants dans la localité qui vendent des repas à emporter.

b Vous cherchez un animal domestique? Cette appli vous montre les personnes dans votre localité qui ont un animal à vendre.

c Vous avez vu un film mais vous avez oublié le nom de la vedette? Pas de problème! On prononce le nom du film et cette appli identifie la vedette.

d Ah non! Panne d'essence! Ne désespérez pas. Cette appli vous montre la station-service la plus proche.

e Des problèmes avec vos devoirs? Cette appli a toutes les informations que vous désirez.

f Est-ce que vos vidéos tremblent ou sont trop sombres? Avec cette appli vous pouvez réparer vos films.

Animapp ☐

Restoquik ☐

Encyclo ☐

Filmsecours ☐

Enroute ☐

Starcherche ☐

4 Choose any three of the descriptions in exercise 3 and translate them into English.

____

____

____

____

____

____

5 Insert the correct forms of the verbs in these conditional sentences.

a Si j'_______ cette appli, je _______ content. (*avoir / être*)

b Si je _______ ANIMAPP, _______ un chat. (*choisir / trouver*)

c Si j'_______ STARCHERCHE, je n'_______ jamais une vedette. (*avoir / oublier*)

d Si Abdou _______ faim, il _______ RESTOQUIK. (*avoir / utiliser*)

e Si Maeva _______ plus de sport, elle _______ contente. (*faire / être*)

f Si Lucas _______ plus d'argent, il _______ à la Martinique. (*avoir / aller*)

g Si j'_______ en ville, je _______ le bus. (*aller / prendre*)

h Si j'_______ cette appli, la vie _______ plus facile. (*utiliser / être*)

6 In pairs. A asks one of the questions below. B replies using a conditional construction. Then swap roles. Try to come up with more questions.

Exemple

A Est-ce que tu as un animal à la maison? **B** Non, mais si j'avais un animal je serais content(e).

a Est-ce que tu as un animal à la maison?
b Tu as faim?
c Tu fais tes devoirs?
d Tu as un appareil-photo?
e Est-ce que tu es riche?
f Est-ce que tu joues au tennis?

7 Read the article and answer the questions. ★

Saviez-vous qu'il y a une appli qui vous aide à écrire un roman? On ajoute les noms des personnages principaux et la ville où se passe l'action. On choisit la catégorie du roman: science-fiction, roman d'amour, roman policier, etc. On décrit la personnalité des personnages et si l'histoire finit bien ou mal. Et voilà – avec un clic, on est devenu auteur. Avec cette appli, vous seriez bientôt aussi célèbre que J.K. Rowling – peut-être!

ROMAN-CLIC

a What does this app help you to do?

____

b List the information you have to input.

____

____

____

____

____

c What could theoretically happen after you've used the app?

____

8 Translate into French. ★

a If I had this app, I would get good marks. _______________

b If Dad had this app, he would learn Spanish. _______________

c If he spoke Spanish, he would go to Spain. _______________

5 Topic 2 Un poème

- Pupil Book pages 106–107

Aujourd' hui est  ______________________. Il est  ______________.

Langue et grammaire

Comparative adverbs

To compare two actions, add *plus* or *moins* before an adverb and use the word *que* to mean 'than':

L'avion vole plus haut que les oiseaux.	The plane flies higher than the birds.
Mon père court moins lentement que ma sœur.	My father runs less slowly than my sister.
Elle danse plus mal que moi!	She dances worse than I do!

To say that one action is performed better than another, use the word *mieux*:

L'oiseau chante mieux que le chien.	The bird sings better than the dog.

Superlative adverbs

To say that someone does something the most, the least or the best, add le before *plus*, *moins* or *mieux*.

Elle écrit le plus souvent.	She writes the most often.
Il court le moins vite.	He runs the least quickly.
C'est elle qui parle le mieux.	She is the best at speaking.

1 Could you write a poem in French? Draw lines to link the words that rhyme.

août	époque
mettent	poisson
suffoque	élite
allons	ajoute
suivre	cœur
chien	nette
quitte	livre
oiseau	enchanté
ordinateur	matin
chanter	rigolo

2 In pairs. A says any French word that comes into his or her head. B must quickly come up with another French word that rhymes with it. Then swap roles.

3 Insert *plus, moins* or *mieux*. The plus and minus signs show what is required.

a Une voiture roule ________ vite qu'un vélo. (+)

b Je parle français ________ que mon père. (+)

c Il parle ________ bien que moi. (–)

d Maeva nage ________ souvent que Félix. (–)

e Je lance le ballon ________ haut que toi. (+)

f Abdou joue bien, mais Sophie joue ________. (+)

g Mon père court ________ vite que moi. (–)

h Mange ________ lentement! (–)

4 Have a boasting competition with your partner. Take turns to read out sentences and give boastful ripostes (using *plus* or *mieux*).

Exemple

A Je cours vite.

B Oui, mais moi, je cours plus vite que toi.

- Je parle bien français.
- Je gagne souvent.
- Je chante bien.
- Je me couche tard.

5 Fill the gaps with *moins, le moins, plus, le plus, mieux* or *le mieux*.

a Félix chante bien, Maeva chante ________, mais Abdou chante ________. (+)

b Je cours vite, mon frère court ________ vite, mais mon père court ________ vite. (+)

c Un lion court vite, un éléphant court ________ vite, mais une tortue court ________ vite. (–)

d Je danse souvent, elle danse ________ souvent, mais tu danses ________ souvent! (–)

e Abdou joue bien, Félix joue ________ bien, mais Sophie joue ________ bien. (–)

f Maman cuisine bien, Papa cuisine ________, mais moi, je cuisine ________! (+)

6 Find expressions in the text meaning:

a yesterday evening ________ b 'A' road ________ c witness ________

d according to ________ e driver ________ f damaged ________

g no one ________ h injured ________

> Hier soir, il y a eu un accident sur la RN 246 près de Cornai. Une Citroën roulait vite, mais une Peugeot roulait encore plus vite (trop vite, selon des témoins) et est entrée en collision avec l'autre voiture. Les témoins ont signalé que le chauffeur de la Peugeot conduisait moins bien que l'autre chauffeur, qui conduisait mieux. La Peugeot a été moins endommagée que la Citroën et heureusement personne n'a été blessé.

7 Re-read the news item in exercise 6 and underline the correct options.

a The accident took place **this morning / yesterday evening**.

b The Citroën was going **faster / slower** than the Peugeot.

c The Peugeot driver was driving **better / worse** than the other driver.

d **Several witnesses / One witness** saw the accident.

e The Citroën was **more / less** damaged than the Peugeot.

f There were **several / no** injuries.

8 Translate the first two sentences of the news item into English. ★

____

____

____

9 Translate these lines into French. With a bit of luck, you should produce a French poem! ★

If I had a big castle

And a swimming pool in the garden

I would eat a big cake

And I would never be hungry.

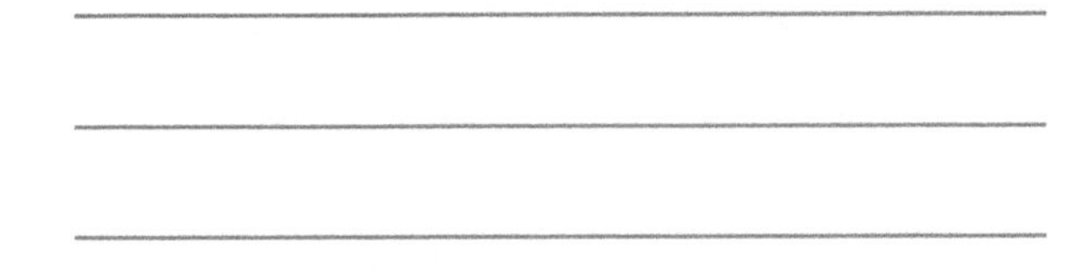

5 Topic 3 Télé ou ordi?

• Pupil Book pages 108–109

Aujourd' hui est  ______________________________. Il est  ____________________.

Langue et grammaire

High numbers and percentages

It is important to make sure you know your numbers well, especially those from seventy to ninety:

70 *soixante-dix*
75 *soixante-quinze*
80 *quatre-vingts*
84 *quatre-vingt-quatre*
90 *quatre-vingt-dix*
94 *quatre-vingt-quatorze*
182 *cent quatre-vingt-deux*

In survey results, percentages are followed by *du*, *de la*, *de l'* or *des*:

soixante-quinze pour cent des ados	75% of teenagers
50% de la population	50% of the population

Par

Remember that *par* can be used to introduce periods of time:

par jour	per day	*par semaine*	per week
par mois	per month	*par an*	per year

In pairs. Are you confident with high numbers? Take turns to point at a number for your partner to say, without hesitation, in French.

Write in *du*, *de la* or *des*.

a 12% ________ ville
b 45% ________ pays
c 73% ________ population
d 95% ________ ados
e 32% ________ voitures
f 21% ________ professeurs
g 5% ________ monde
h 15% ________ émissions

Translate into French.

a twice a day deux fois par jour

b three times a week ______

c eight times a month ______

d twelve times a year ______

e once an hour ______

Choose words from the box to fill in the gaps.

télécharge	recherches	rattrapage	vidéos	tutoriels	émission

a Je fais des ______ pour mes devoirs.

b Demain, je regarderai des ______.

c Manon ______ de la musique.

d J'apprends à jouer de la guitare avec des ______.

e L'______ commence à huit heures.

f J'utilise la télé de ______.

5 Underline the correct option according to the text.

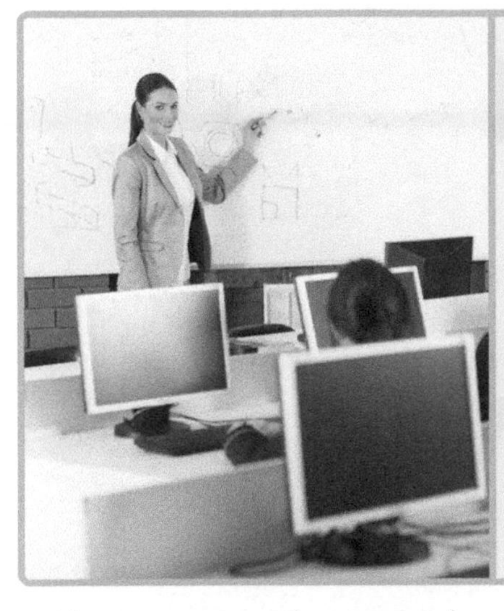

Les profs de technologie du Collège Jean-Jaurès ont fait un sondage sur les élèves et les médias. On a posé des questions à cent élèves entre 12 et 14 ans. Voici les résultats.

- 92% possèdent un portable.
- 83% surfent sur Internet pendant la récré.
- 79% utilisent des réseaux sociaux.
- 75% utilisent une tablette tactile pour leurs études.
- 54% utilisent la télé de rattrapage.
- 20% ont regardé une vidéo violente.
- 18% regardent la télé le soir avec leurs parents.
- 11% ont envoyé un SMS pendant les cours!

a How many pupils use catch-up TV? a lot / not many / about half

b How many watch TV with their parents? a lot / not many / about half

c How many have a mobile phone? a lot / not many / about half

d How many have seen a violent video? a lot / not many / about half

e How many use social media? a lot / not many / about half

f How many go online at break time? a lot / not many / about half

g How many admit to sending texts in lessons? a lot / not many / about half

h How many use a tablet for studying? a lot / not many / about half

6 Read the text. Are the sentences below the text true or false? Write *vrai* or *faux*.

Pour Noël, Maman m'a acheté une tablette tactile. Cet appareil est plus grand qu'un portable mais plus petit qu'un ordinateur. Maman avait peur que je passe des heures à jouer à des jeux vidéo et à communiquer avec mes copains sur les réseaux sociaux. Et c'est vrai! Mais il y a d'autres avantages. Par exemple, je peux faire des recherches pour m'aider avec mes études au lycée. Et je peux utiliser la télé de rattrapage. Comme ça, Maman peut regarder la télé dans le salon pendant que moi, je regarde une autre émission que j'ai enregistrée hier. Voilà, tout le monde est content.

a Laurent a acheté une tablette pour sa mère. ______

b Une tablette est plus grande qu'un portable. ______

c Laurent n'aime pas les jeux vidéo. ______

d Il utilise les réseaux sociaux pour communiquer avec ses amis. ______

e Sa tablette peut l'aider à l'école. ______

f Laurent regarde la télé dans le salon. ______

g Il utilise la télé de rattrapage. ______

h Maman est contente. ______

7 Translate the text in exercise 6 into English from *Mais il y a…* to the end. ★

8 Write a few lines about how you use TV and social media. Use expressions of time and vary the tenses to describe things you **will do** and **have done**. ★

5 Topic 4 Au spectacle

- Pupil Book pages 110–111

Aujourd' hui est  ________________________. Il est  __________________.

Langue et grammaire

Qui

Remember that *qui* is a relative pronoun used to link two parts of a sentence. It can refer to things as well as people and can mean 'that' or 'who' depending on the context.

*Elle est amoureuse d'un étudiant **qui** s'appelle Marius.*	She is in love with a student **who** is called Marius.
*C'est un film **qui** dure deux heures.*	It's a film **that** lasts two hours.

The passive

The passive voice is used to express an action that is done to someone or something. You will recognise the passive when you see the relevant form of *être* followed by the past participle of the verb used. The passive can be used in different tenses.

Present tense

*La chanson **est chantée** par Fantine.*	The song is sung by Fantine.

Past tense

*Le livre **a été traduit** en japonais.*	The book was translated into Japanese.

Future tense

*Le programme **sera préparé** par les élèves.*	The programme will be prepared by pupils.

1 Decide whether these sentences are active (A) or passive (P).

a Kylie chante une chanson. ☐

b Une fille a été maltraitée. ☐

c Le livre a été traduit. ☐

d Jean a aidé Fantine. ☐

e On a traduit le livre. ☐

f Fantine a été aidée. ☐

g Une chanson est chantée par Kylie. ☐

h Les Thénardier ont maltraité une fille. ☐

2 Join these sentences together using *qui*.

a C'est une fille. Elle a une enfance difficile. ____________________

b J'aime le film. Il est très célèbre. ____________________

c Marius est un étudiant. Il est riche. ____________________

d Gavroche est un garçon. Il est souvent dans la rue. ____________________

e Victor Hugo était un écrivain. Il a écrit *Les Misérables.* ____________________

f J'ai acheté un livre. Il est très connu. ____________________

Notre-Dame de Paris est un autre roman célèbre de Victor Hugo. Ce roman a été écrit en 1831. Le titre fait référence à la cathédrale de Paris, qui est le lieu principal de ce roman. Le personnage le plus connu est Quasimodo, un homme qui est sourd et boiteux. Quasimodo, qui a été abandonné par ses parents, est amoureux d'Esmeralda. Esmeralda est une jeune gitane de seize ans qui danse dans les rues près de la cathédrale. Elle est très innocente et belle, et elle aime Phœbus de Châteaupers, un capitaine de la garde. Claude Frollo, qui est l'archidiacre de la cathédrale, adore Esmeralda mais elle le déteste. Pierre Gringoire est un artiste pauvre qui se marie avec Esmeralda. C'est une histoire compliquée mais très populaire.

3 Identify these people.

a The archdeacon of Notre-Dame ______________________

b A beautiful gypsy girl ______________________

c The man who marries Esmeralda ______________________

d A man who is deaf ______________________

e A military man ______________________

f A famous author ______________________

4 Re-read the text in exercise 3 and answer these questions.

a When was the book written? ______________________

b What is *Notre-Dame de Paris*? ______________________

c Whom does he love? ______________________

d How is she described? ______________________

e How does she feel about Claude Frollo? ______________________

f Who is Pierre Gringoire? ______________________

g How is the story described? ______________________

5 Draw a ring round any passive sentences in the text in exercise 3 and underline any sentences that include a relative pronoun (*qui*).

6 Translate the last two paragraphs of the text in exercise 3 (starting *Esmeralda est...*) into English. ★

____

____

____

____

____

____

7 Translate into French. ★

a She's a girl who loves an artist.

____

b He's a man who lives in Paris.

____

c The book was written by Victor Hugo.

____

d Quasimodo was played by Anthony Quinn.

____

8 Write as much as you can in French about any book you have read (even if it isn't a French book!). Try to use *qui* and a couple of passive sentences. ★

____

____

____

____

5 Topic 5 L'école du cirque

• Pupil Book pages 112–113

Aujourd' hui est ______________________________. Il est ______________________.

Langue et grammaire

Vous

Remember the *vous* form of verbs always ends in *–ez*, regardless of the tense or whether the verb is active or passive.

*Vous av**ez***	You have
*Vous av**iez***	You used to have
*Vous aur**ez***	You will have
*Vous conseill**ez***	You advise
*Vous ser**iez***	You would be

There are only two exceptions:

Vous êtes	You are
Vous faites	You do / are doing / make / are making

Asking questions

When asking formal questions, pay attention to the word order. The verb comes before the subject.

Quand avez-vous commencé?	When did you start?
Quelles sont vos qualités?	What are your qualities?
Pourquoi avez-vous peur?	Why are you scared?

The word order is different if you introduce the question with *est-ce que* or *qu'est-ce que*.

Est-ce que vous jonglez?	Do you juggle?
Qu'est-ce que vous préférez?	What do you prefer?

Read the clues and fill in the grid with vocabulary from this topic. What is the mystery word in the tinted boxes down?

1 □□□□□

2 □□□

3 □□□□□□□

4 □□□□□□□□□

5 □□□□□□

6 □□□□□□□

1 lessons
2 rope
3 fun
4 balance
5 to attend (lessons)
6 to juggle

The mystery word is ______________ .

2 Change these verbs from the *tu* form into the *vous* form.

a tu as ________

b tu joueras ________

c tu fais ________

d tu regarderas ________

e tu travaillais ________

f tu jouais ________

g tu avais ________

h tu jongles ________

i tu serais ________

j tu es ________

k tu aurais ________

l tu vas ________

m tu iras ________

n tu ferais ________

3 Identify the tense of each verb in exercise 2. In the box, write P (present), I (imperfect), F (future) or C (conditional).

4 Unjumble these formal questions. You will have to insert a hyphen.

a arrivé? vous Quand êtes ________

b êtes triste? Pourquoi vous ________

c vous au allez lycée? Comment ________

d voulez Où manger? vous ________

e vous Quel pris? Avez train ________

f Pourquoi vous la restez à maison? ________

5 Translate into French.

a That must be difficult. ________

b That must be tiring. ________

c That must be fun. ________

d That must be great. ________

e That must be fantastic. ________

6 In pairs. A mentions a circus skill and B replies with a comment beginning Ça doit être… Then swap roles.

Exemple

A J'aime jongler.

B Ça doit être difficile.

Read the advert and answer the questions.

a When will the circus be in town?

____

b What kinds of acts will be on show?

____

____

c What will the clowns do?

____

d What else will be on show?

____

e What are you encouraged to do?

____

Translate this conversation into English. ★

____

____

____

____

____

____

____

5 Topic 6 La musique

- Pupil Book pages 114–115

Aujourd' hui est  ______________________. Il est  ______________.

Langue et grammaire

The subjunctive

Some phrases expressing wish or command, such as *il faut que* and *vouloir que*, are followed by a form of the verb called the subjunctive. The endings of the subjunctive are straightforward:

pronoun	ending
je	*–e*
tu	*–es*
il/elle/on	*–e*
nous	*–ions*
vous	*–iez*
ils/elles	*–ent*

Je voudrais que tu parles mieux.	I would like you to speak better.
Il faut que vous regardiez ce spectacle.	You should watch this show.

However, some common verbs use a different stem for the subjunctive, and in the case of *avoir* and *être* some of the endings are irregular too.

avoir to have	***être*** to be	***faire*** to do, to make
que j'aie	*que je sois*	*que je fasse*
que tu aies	*que tu sois*	*que tu fasses*
qu'il/elle/on ait	*qu'il/elle/on soit*	*qu'il/elle/on fasse*
que nous ayons	*que nous soyons*	*que nous fassions*
que vous ayez	*que vous soyez*	*que vous fassiez*
qu'ils/elles aient	*qu'ils/elles soient*	*qu'ils/elles fassent*
aller to go	***venir*** to come	***savoir*** to know
que j'aille	*que je vienne*	*que je sache*
que tu ailles	*que tu viennes*	*que tu saches*
qu'il/elle/on aille	*qu'il/elle/on vienne*	*qu'il/elle/on sache*
que nous allions	*que nous venions*	*que nous sachions*
que vous alliez	*que vous veniez*	*que vous sachiez*
qu'ils/elles aillent	*qu'ils/elles viennent*	*qu'ils/elles sachent*

 **1** Each of these sentences contains a subjunctive verb. Underline it.

a Il faut que la réponse soit bonne.

b Je ne veux pas que ma mère sache que je fume.

c Je voudrais que tu viennes en ville avec moi.

d Il faut que nous allions au concert.

e Je ne veux pas que tu aies peur.

f Il faut que je fasse mes devoirs.

 **2** Tick indicative or subjunctive.

verb	indicative	subjunctive	verb	indicative	subjunctive
a il sait	☐	☐	b nous avons	☐	☐
c on soit	☐	☐	d il sache	☐	☐
e elle a	☐	☐	f on est	☐	☐
g nous ayons	☐	☐	h elle ait	☐	☐
i je viens	☐	☐	j tu viennes	☐	☐

Find words for describing music in this grid. There are ten words and they mean: dynamic, animated, noisy, rhythmic, dark, sad, calm, sinister, moving and poetic.

b	r	u	y	a	n	t	p	a	i	q	u	e	j
u	m	w	g	n	m	v	v	é	i	n	h	e	i
k	f	g	e	i	s	b	q	m	e	w	e	j	d
f	t	r	à	m	l	y	u	o	u	h	i	l	d
p	h	p	o	é	t	i	q	u	e	r	m	o	y
o	z	v	l	b	z	a	n	v	m	n	é	é	n
c	d	n	f	r	r	c	c	a	l	m	e	w	a
é	m	o	p	o	b	d	j	n	o	r	t	t	m
u	s	q	s	i	n	i	s	t	r	e	b	l	i
t	p	o	é	o	e	y	o	s	l	à	q	u	q
u	i	m	r	y	t	h	m	i	q	u	e	b	u
i	v	s	f	f	c	g	b	t	r	i	s	t	e
c	a	l	o	m	d	h	r	r	l	q	u	k	j
g	w	x	n	é	e	a	e	l	r	h	y	a	p

4 In pairs. One partner thinks of a type of music, using an adjective from exercise 3. The other asks questions to guess what it is. Then swap roles.

Exemple

A C'est de la musique triste?

B Non.

A C'est de la musique rythmique?

B Oui, c'est ça!

Read the article and answer the questions.

Daft Punk est un duo français qui a gagné le prix Grammy en 2014 avec son album Random Access Memories et le single de l'année pour 'Get Lucky'. Daft Punk a été créé en 1993 et comprend deux Parisiens, Guy-Manuel de Homem-Christo et Thomas Bangalter. Leur premier album s'appelait Homework. Leur musique, du genre House, est dansante, dynamique, animée et rythmique. En scène, leur spectacle est très visuel. Le duo se déguise en robots. Vous voulez faire une interview avec Daft Punk? Pas de chance! Les artistes ne donnent pas d'interviews et passent rarement.

a Where do Daft Punk come from? ______________________

b What was their award-winning single? ______________________

c When was the group formed? ______________________

d What was their first album called? ______________________

e What style is their music? ____________________

f How are their live shows described? ____________________

g What image do they like to portray? ____________________

h What is unusual about them for big stars? ____________________

6 Choose one of the subjunctive verbs from the box to fill in each gap.

sache alliez viennes

a Il faut que vous ________ voir Daft Punk. C'est un spectacle incroyable!

b Je voudrais que tu ________ avec moi au Palais Bercy pour voir Daft Punk.

c Je ne veux pas que ma mère ________ que je vais au concert.

7 Translate the text in exercise 5 into English from *Leur musique…* to the end. ★

____

____

____

____

____

8 Using the exercise 5 text as a model, write about a rock or pop act you like. Try to extend your work by using a range of tenses, descriptions and opinions. Use the skills you have learned in *Mission: français. Bonne chance!* ★

____

____

____

____

____

Notes